An Atlas of
Poverty in America

An Atlas of Poverty in America

One Nation, Pulling Apart, 1960–2003

Amy K. Glasmeier

Routledge
Taylor & Francis Group
New York   London

This research was supported by a grant from The Ford Foundation. The research team appreciates the Foundation's support. The Ford Foundation is not responsible for the content of and opinions expressed in this analysis.

Published in 2006 by
Routledge
Taylor & Francis Group
270 Madison Avenue
New York, NY 10016

Published in Great Britain by
Routledge
Taylor & Francis Group
2 Park Square
Milton Park, Abingdon
Oxon OX14 4RN

Printed in the United States of America on acid-free paper
10 9 8 7 6 5 4 3 2 1

International Standard Book Number-10: 0-415-95335-9 (Hardcover) 0-415-95336-7 (Softcover)
International Standard Book Number-13: 978-0-415-95335-1 (Hardcover) 978-0-415-95336-8 (Softcover)
Library of Congress Card Number 2005028141

Library of Congress Cataloging-in-Publication Data

Glasmeier, Amy.
    An atlas of poverty in America : one nation, pulling apart, 1960-2003 / Amy K. Glasmeier.
        p. cm.
    Includes bibliographical references and index.
    ISBN 0-415-95335-9 (hb) -- ISBN 0-415-95336-7 (pb)
    1. Poverty--United States--History--20th century. 2. Poverty--United States--History--21st century. 3. Poverty--United States--History--Atlases. 4. Regional economic disparities--United States--History--20th century. 5. Regional economic disparities--United States--History--21st century. 6. Regional economic disparities--United States--History--Atlases. I. Title: Poverty in America. II. Title.

HC110.P6G543 2005
339.4'6097309045--dc22
        2005028141

Taylor & Francis Group is the Academic Division of Informa plc.

Visit the Taylor & Francis Web site at
http://www.taylorandfrancis.com

and the Routledge Web site at
http://www.routledge-ny.com

Contributions to the Atlas

We have many people to thank for their support of and assistance with this Atlas. These include our funder, The Ford Foundation, and Mil Duncan and Michael Conroy, program officers; the members of the project; Penn State; the College of Earth and Mineral Sciences; the Department of Geography; the Earth and Environmental Systems Institute; the Dutton e-Education Institute; the Population Research Institute; the National Archives; the Inter-University Consortium for Social and Political Science Research; the U.S. Bureau of the Census; the Appalachian Regional Commission; The Mumford Center at the University of Albany; and many others.

This project could not have been accomplished without the remarkable efforts of a great group of people who have worked on the One Nation project for more than three years. Special recognition goes to four people: Tom Bell, Lee Carpenter, Tracey Farrigan, and Phil Kolb.

Tom Bell stepped into the breach and created the tool that would become the basis of the Atlas. Had it not been for his ability to create an easy-to-use mapping tool that allowed me to conduct the original cartographic study of poverty in America, the Atlas would never have happened. His subsequent dogged determination to extract the most obscure data from various places and incorporate them into the mapping system made the Atlas a treasure trove of data.

Sherilee Carpenter (aka Lee) has been with the project from its conception. She has served many critical roles from project facilitator, to editor, to Atlas project manager. Lee has been the fulcrum around which the Atlas has developed. Her constant attention to detail, her understanding of document preparation, and her sensibilities about story-telling to appeal to a broad audience have made the Atlas accessible and accurate. Any remaining errors are my own.

Tracey Farrigan deserves special thanks for the work she did on the One Nation project. Throughout the project she occupied many roles, including project analyst, writer, and content contributor. Tracey built the Living Wage Tool, wrote many of the policy histories, conducted the impact studies, developed the Economic Development Library, and pushed the envelope of ideas that became many of the end products of the project.

Phil Kolb joined the project in the latter third of its life. Once he was brought on board, the Atlas began to take shape and became the visual product it is today. There were many challenges in this exercise, from translating existing graphical material into a uniform format, to making original maps with a wide variety of data, to developing the overall color scheme, to considering how to visually integrate the history of poverty of America over the decades. Phil took on a project that became much greater in size and scale than our original vision. His talents are evident on each page.

This is very much a product of a joint collaboration among truly talented people and I am grateful for having had the opportunity to work with and learn from them.

The research and support team has had a life of its own and cannot be thanked enough. It also included, in alphabetical order: David DiBiase, Director of the Dutton e-Education Institute, who provided institutional support for the Atlas project; Emily Dux, index checker; Shaun Faith, cartographic and design reviewer; Erin Heithoff, original layout and graphical designer; Christy Jocoy, analyst; Debbie Lambert, staff assistant; Mike Norad, creator of Tech-Base; Martin Shields, author of the toolbox and applied economist; Sue Rockey, budget analyst and financial officer; Larry Wood, analyst and expert on the Appalachian Regional Commission; and Scott Woods, web site designer, analytical tool developer, all-around superb programmer, and fearless rock climber. Cindy Brewer of Penn State and Trudy Suchan of the Census and others gave graphics advice. Ron Johnston of the University of Bristol, and Mary Anne Carr and Matt Lee read the Atlas for content, argument, and clarity. They are not responsible for the final product. Added to these intimate colleagues are all the people around the nation we were able to consult with about data, questions of representation, history, and the underlying information system describing the topics presented here.

Table of Contents

List of Tables, Figures, Maps, and Photographs

Photographs

History of the Atlas Project

This Atlas has been written to provide an historical and contemporary account of economic opportunity in the United States. The United States is a nation pulling apart to a degree unknown in the last twenty-five years. A decade of strong national economic growth in the 1990s left many of America's communities falling far behind median national measures of economic health. Despite the investments in transportation and public facilities infrastructures, massive movements of capital and people, and the expectations of most regional economists over the past forty years, the nation's regional development patterns are becoming more uneven. The number of communities falling behind the national economic average is increasing. This tendency has been most pronounced in recent years, when trade liberalization and globalization have greatly opened the American economy.

According to our estimates in 2003, almost 25% of the nation's counties had low per-capita incomes below one half the national average or less, high unemployment, low labor force participation rates, and a high dependency on government transfer payments—all measures of economic distress. These communities are located in timber, agricultural, and mineral and energy resource areas in the nation and in regions of the deep South including the Mississippi Delta, the eastern coal belt of Appalachia, historic New Mexican and Native American communities, and along our borders. More recently, newly distressed counties are experiencing the collapse of their post-war low-wage manufacturing economies. At a smaller spatial scale, communities in persistent poverty also are present in the nation's cities, where long-term decline has left core urban areas of cities such as Washington, DC, Detroit, Michigan, and Los Angeles, California with limited job opportunities, high levels of poverty, and populations with few effective means of economic advancement.

The problem of persistent poverty is a complex one that includes communities and individuals who, through no fault of their own, find themselves unable to make ends meet in this globalizing, information-intensive world. People at risk are women, children, and people of color, single-parent families, and the elderly. Large numbers of the nation's citizens live at or below the poverty threshold, which means each month is a struggle to pay the bills and provide the basics, including food, clothing, and shelter, not to mention access to health care and simple comforts. How can the richest country in the world still have more than 12% of its total population, and almost 20% of all children under the age of 18, unable to meet, let alone be guaranteed coverage of, basic needs?

Today, as a nation, we are significantly different than we were in 1960, when more than 20% of the population was visibly poor and lacked basic goods, including food, clothing, proper shelter, clean water, heating, health care, and access to decent schools. We are a more diverse population and a more dispersed population; we are older and remain divided by race, income, and location. Certainly progress has been made over the intervening forty years in terms of an overall minimum standard of living as measured by material conditions. And yet the lived experience of poor people is starkly different from that of individuals and families who enjoy some degree of economic security as measured by income levels that provide comfortable, worry-free circumstances. If anything, the gap between the economically secure and the poor is more severe than it was four decades ago. Increasingly, the nation is composed of persons who look to a future in which circumstances include the expectation of more wealth, security, and opportunity; and the alternative, those who struggle to make ends meet. In many families today, children cannot say they expect to be better off than their parents. This is perhaps the greatest challenge now facing our society.

Forty years ago, public officials took a stand against economic deprivation. For a short period of time we made huge strides in reducing economic insecurity. America is again facing this serious challenge. Once again we can make a difference if we choose to look this issue in the eye.

Why an Atlas about Poverty?

This volume is one of many that has been written since 1970, calling national attention to a concern for economic opportunity and justice. The history of America is complex but its roots are in two often compelling, yet conflicting visions of a social contract. America is founded on the view that it is a nation where everyone deserves a chance and is responsible for his- or herself. By mapping poverty as both a process and outcome through time, we can see the enduring nature of its existence and its peculiar persistence. By mapping it through time and with attention to geographic location we can and do find the answer to one of the most important challenges our nation continues to face today, which is this: in a nation of such wealth and opportunity, why do some people and places fail to succeed? What is it about how our nation is constituted that has such stark differences in outcome? By knowing where we fall short and where more needs to be done, can we resolve this important challenge?

The topics displayed in this Atlas were selected based on many factors, most importantly the historical record of poverty in America and the lived experience of being poor in our nation today. A central theme is the enduring character of poverty in America, consistently affecting groups of individuals and places over time. A key message of this Atlas is that America's poor are people who work or who are dependents of people who work and face limited opportunity, often due to living in places that are seriously disadvantaged because of geography or history or both. The story also is one about public policy and the extent to which public intervention has been sufficient to ensure that all persons in this country have an equal chance to achieve their highest potential.

Point of Departure

What does poverty, being poor, economic insecurity, low-wage work, working poor, and inability to make ends meet, mean?

This Atlas is based on a group of ideas about economic well-being in America. We use the terms poverty, being poor, economic insecurity, low-wage work, working poor, and unable to make ends meet to reflect a state or condition of being in which an individual, an age cohort, or a group in society lacks the ability to enjoy life due to lack of access to basic needs such as food, clothing, shelter, health care, and essential requirements for a successful work life such as a decent education and access to a vehicle. Many additional activities of daily living, such as entertainment, eating out, vacations, and retirement, which many of us take for granted, are unavailable to large numbers of persons who are not regarded as income-poor but yet do not have the discretionary income to enjoy these forms of entertainment. Such issues are not considered in this analysis and people are not assumed to expect or have access to such elements as part of their quality of life.

How We Define Poverty in This Atlas

Being poor or in poverty means that you receive or earn insufficient income to pay for necessities of daily living. Here we define poverty as understood in America based on two frameworks—poverty thresholds and poverty guidelines.

Poverty Thresholds

In the mid-1960s, after much debate within the federal government, the first official measure of poverty was developed in 1963–1964 by Molly Orshansky of the Social Security Administration. At the time, poverty was considered transitory. The belief was that people experienced poverty on a temporary basis. Individuals and families would emerge from poverty upon achieving full employment. Orshansky developed poverty thresholds based on a food plan created by the U.S. Department of Agriculture. Her measure was based on the

USDA's 1955 Household Food Consumption Survey (the latest available survey at the time), that is the amount of income spent by families on food. The food plan was "designed for temporary or emergency use when funds were low," according to the USDA. Orshansky knew that families of three or more persons spent about one third of their after-tax income on food. Taking this information, she then multiplied the cost of the USDA economy food plan by three to arrive at the minimal yearly income for a family. Using 1963 as a base year, she calculated that a family of four (two adults and two children) would spend $1,033 on food/year. Using her formula based on the 1955 survey, she arrived at $3,100 a year ($1,033 x 3) as the poverty threshold for a family of four in 1963.

The original thresholds differentiated by family size, by farm/non-farm status, by the number of family members who were children, by gender of the head of household, and by aged/non-aged status. The result was a detailed matrix of 124 poverty thresholds. Generally, the figures cited were weighted average thresholds for each family size.

Evolution of the Poverty Measure

In 1965, the Johnson administration's Office of Economic Opportunity adopted Orshansky's poverty thresholds as a working definition of poverty. In the late 1960s, Social Security Administration policymakers and analysts expressed concern about how to adjust the poverty thresholds for increases in the standard of living. Inflation had increased over the decade and there was a growing recognition that the measure no longer accurately reflected the cost of living. In 1969, the poverty thresholds were revaluated and adjusted for price changes, and not for changes in the general standard of living. It also was decided at the time that the thresholds would be indexed by the Consumer Price Index rather than the per-capita cost of the thrifty food plan. The Bureau of the Budget—now the Office of Management and Budget—designated the poverty thresholds, with their revisions, as the federal government's official statistical definition of poverty.

Over the ensuing decades, various committees and task forces have been formed to explore the question of whether the poverty thresholds need to be adjusted and how that might be done. In 1992, the National Research Council of the National Academies of Science appointed a Panel on Poverty and Family Assistance to conduct a study on the measurement of poverty. During this investigation a number of adjustments to the existing poverty measure were explored. In this Atlas, we explore this redefinition in the section on elderly poverty.

Measuring Poverty Today

Each year, the U.S. Census Bureau updates the poverty threshold to account for inflation. The estimated 2004 threshold value of $19,484 for a family of four represents the same purchasing power as the threshold value of $3,100 in 1963 (Table 1).

Poverty thresholds by number of related children age <18 and size of family, 2004									
	Number of children age <18								
Size of family unit	0	1	2	3	4	5	6	7	8+
1 person (unrelated individuals)									
Age <65	9,827								
Age 65+	9,060								
2 persons									
Householder age <65	12,649	13,020							
Householder age 65+	11,418	12,971							
3 persons	14,776	15,205	15,219						
4 persons	19,484	19,803	19,157	19,223					
5 persons	23,497	23,838	23,108	22,543	22,199				
6 persons	27,025	27,133	26,573	26,037	25,241	24,768			
7 persons	31,096	31,290	30,621	30,154	29,285	28,271	27,159		
8 persons	34,778	35,086	34,454	33,901	33,115	32,119	31,082	30,818	
9 persons or more	41,836	42,039	41,480	41,010	40,240	39,179	38,220	37,983	36,520

Table 1. *Poverty level for a family of four is less than $20,000*

The Practical Side of Poverty Measurement

Poverty guidelines are a simplification of the poverty thresholds for administrative purposes, such as determining the financial eligibility for certain federal programs. The U.S. Department of Health and Human Services issues poverty guidelines each year in the *Federal Register*. Poverty guidelines are designated by their year of issue. Poverty guidelines are often commonly called the "federal poverty level" or "federal poverty line."

Strengths and Weaknesses of the Official Poverty Measure

We acknowledge that the federal measure of poverty has been subject to critique by researchers and policymakers alike for many years. The current measure does not include income either direct or in-kind received by low-income people in the form of public assistance.

Second, the poverty line is dependent on income as a measure of sufficiency. The poverty line is based on gross earnings before taxes. It is unadjusted for differences in costs of living among different places. Families may be unable to meet their basic needs with the income they bring home, but they will not be counted as poor if their before-tax income is above the poverty threshold. In this way, the current U.S. poverty rates may underestimate poverty among the working poor.

Third, the poverty measure still assumes that families spend about one third of their income on food. This is no longer the case. Food makes up about one sixth of expenditures. Housing, utilities, and transportation are a much larger share of expenses today than in the 1960s. Other expenses thought critical in today's households where both adults work, such as childcare, also are not included. Incorporating transportation, health care, and childcare expenses suggest the official poverty measure understates the minimum level of income for a family of four by 100% (Figure 1).

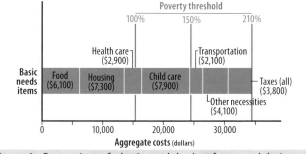

Figure 1. *Comparison of a basic needs budget for two adults/two children and the poverty thresholds*

Fourth, the poverty measure is based on an absolute rather than a relative standard. A poor family today is much worse off, relative to the average family, than a poor family was in the 1960s. This is because the living standards of the median family have increased dramatically over the past thirty-five years, while the poverty thresholds still assume that families need only three times their basic food needs. In countries such as Britain and Sweden, the poverty line is set at a given proportion of the median income rather than reflecting a fixed amount of money. For example, families with incomes below 50% of the median family income (adjusted for family size) are classified as poor in these countries.

Recognizing these limitations, we use the federal poverty measure because it is comparable across time and locations and is readily available from government statistical sources.

Additional Metrics of Opportunity

In this Atlas we also address the issue of the growing significance of Americans who work but who are poor by income standards. Over the last thirty years the number of jobs that do not pay a wage that lifts a family of four above the poverty level has increased dramatically. Today, as many as 25% of all jobs pay less than a poverty-level income. While historically the majority of persons defined as poor in the U.S. have worked, the steady growth in jobs that do not pay a living wage presents new challenges for society. When we use the term "working but poor", we are describing an individual or family in which an individual is employed at least 27 weeks a year and would work more if employment was available.

We also use the term "living wage" in conjunction with the discussion of the working poor. A living wage is a wage level that takes into account differences in the cost of living across locations. In many areas of the country the national minimum wage of $5.15/hour provides an after-tax income insufficient to support individuals or families.

Finally, in a number of sections in the Atlas we examine the distribution of income in the United States. Over the last forty years the distribution of income in the country has become more unequal, with an increasingly larger share of total income accruing to the top 5% of individuals and families. The same is true for the distribution of wealth and financial assets. A simple measure that economists use to express inequality is called the GINI coefficient, which is a number that varies between zero and one. It varies from zero, which indicates perfect equality, with every household earning exactly the same, to one, which implies absolute inequality, with a single household earning a country's entire income. Latin America, the region with the most unequal income in the world, has a GINI coefficient of around 0.50; in most industrialized countries the figure is closer to 0.30. In the U.S. the number is approaching 0.50 (Figure 2).

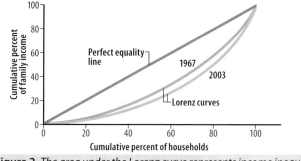

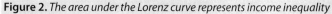
Figure 2. *The area under the Lorenz curve represents income inequality*

The Lorenz curve is a graphical representation of inequality. It measures the extent to which the distribution of an indicator of interest, in our case, income, is equally distributed in a population. In the case of income in the U.S, if we array the population in equal size intervals of 20% of the population (referred to as quintiles), perfect equality would be found when households in each quintile received an equal share of national household income. The further the Lorenz curve lies below the line of equality, the more unequal is the distribution of income. The graph shows that during 2003, the bottom 20% of households in the United States (groups of people living together, usually families, or single people if they live alone) had total incomes of less than 3.4% of total household income. The top quintile received 49.8% of total household income, respectively. If we compare 1967 data and 2003 data we can see the significant change in distribution of income.

How to Read This Atlas

This Atlas rests on literary and graphical conventions that are customary in atlases. These conventions include the scale of geographical representation (place, city, county, region, state, nation), the numerical scale adopted to reflect trends in the conditions or places studied, the time scale, the color scheme used to show differences among places and across time, the numbering of captions, and the referencing of sources.

Figures, maps, photos, and tables are numbered sequentially through the Atlas. Each graphic appears shortly after it is referred to in the text and is followed by its caption.

Sources of data come from hundreds of publications, groups, and individuals who study the various themes in this Atlas. The sections each have sources, which are referred to at the end of the Atlas. In addition, the project web site has a web-linked version of the Atlas with hyperlinks to the sources current to the date of Atlas publication.

Although the data are drawn from many sources, the backbone of this Atlas is the U.S. Census from 1959–2000. The early census data were acquired thanks to the Appalachian Regional Commission, the federal state cooperating agency set up in 1964 to help reduce poverty in one of the nation's poorest regions, Appalachia. The 1970 Census was acquired from the National Archives in Washington, DC. The data are stored in a three-dimensional database that can be analyzed using any number of programs, but importantly is available in a geographic analysis system that makes possible complex queries that can be displayed in maps at multiple spatial scales by virtually anyone regardless of their ability to make maps. There is an accompanying data warehouse and tool kit that allows individuals and organizations to analyze their local economies for any number of purposes.

Unit of Analysis

An important convention adopted throughout this Atlas is our analysis of poverty condition at the county level. Most studies of poverty incidence in the U.S. examine the average of the individual in tandem with the rate of poverty based on the number of individuals for whom poverty-level income is known. While this measure of economic condition is an important starting point, people exist in places, and poverty is a condition experienced in those locations. In this Atlas our goal is to consider simultaneously individual circumstances and those circumstances in places where people are located. Forty years of poverty policy underscores the point that poverty is both a people and a place concern. As the evidence in this Atlas demonstrates, place poverty is persistent over time and in some cases has increased in severity across the last four decades.

Our goal in using data reflecting conditions over time was to include as much about temporal change as possible given constraints regarding changes in data definitions, geographic boundaries, and numerical representations of information. Much of what we had to draw upon came from the census and conventions changed through time and these definitional changes sometimes acted as constraints. Wherever possible we sought uniformity of information across time.

The data are mapped by percent of a condition or in dollars relative to the county or state. Income data are adjusted for inflation to constant 2003 dollars.

How to Interpret the Maps

Maps that refer to one group of people in one location at one point in time are shown by using a 5-class sequential color scheme. The average value of this data set is used as a class break and highlighted in the legend (Map 1). Pairs of maps that compare data between two groups of people or time periods are shown by using a six-class sequential color scheme with both averages being used as class breaks (Map 2). This style is also used for single maps that display a second average for comparison (Map 3).

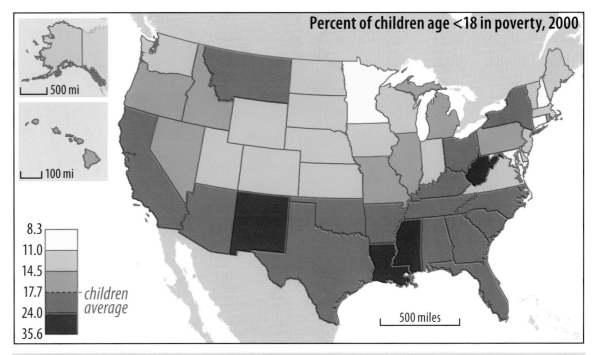

Percent of children age <18 in poverty, 2000

500 mi
100 mi

8.3
11.0
14.5
17.7 - - - - children
24.0   average
35.6

500 miles

Map 1. *Children in poverty in 2000. Map showing average of 17.7%.*

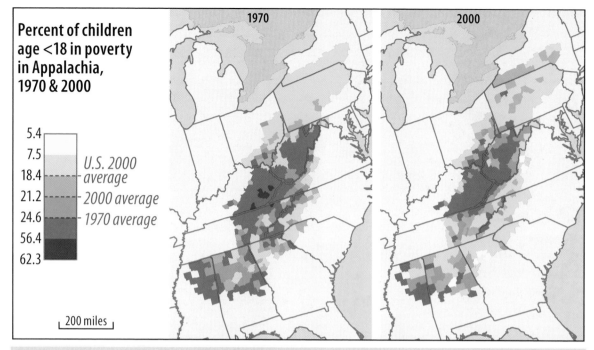

Percent of children age <18 in poverty in Appalachia, 1970 & 2000

1970

2000

5.4
7.5
18.4
21.2
24.6
56.4
62.3

U.S. 2000 average
2000 average
1970 average

200 miles

Map 2. *Children in Appalachia in 1970 & 2000. Map showing a 1970 average of 24.6% and a 2000 average of 21.2%.*

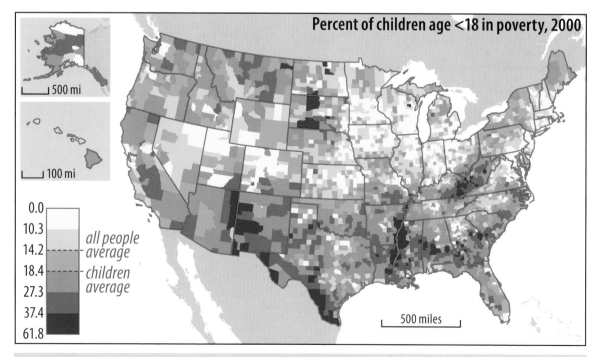

Percent of children age <18 in poverty, 2000

500 mi

100 mi

0.0
10.3
14.2
18.4
27.3
37.4
61.8

all people average
children average

500 miles

Map 3. *Children in the U.S. in 2000. Map showing an average for children of 18.4% and an average for all people of 14.2%.*

Basics of Poverty

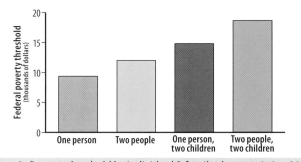

Figure 3. *Poverty threshold by individual & family characteristics, 2003*

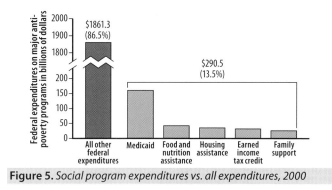

Figure 5. *Social program expenditures vs. all expenditures, 2000*

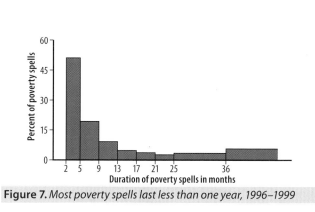

Figure 7. *Most poverty spells last less than one year, 1996–1999*

Percent of persons below the poverty level by race and ethnicity, 2003

Race	Total	Number below poverty level	Percentage below poverty level
White	231,866	24,272	10.5%
Black	40,300	9,051	22.5
Hispanic	35,989	8,781	24.4
Asian and Pacific Islander	11,856	1,401	11.8

Numbers in thousands

Table 2. *Race and ethnicity of people in poverty, 2003*

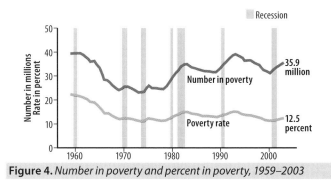

Figure 4. *Number in poverty and percent in poverty, 1959–2003*

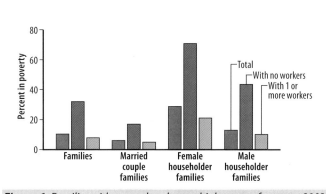

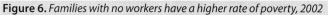

Figure 6. *Families with no workers have a higher rate of poverty, 2002*

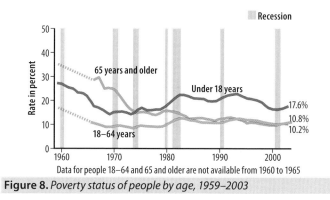

Figure 8. *Poverty status of people by age, 1959–2003*

Introduction: *The Paradox of Poverty in America*

American society is based on paradoxes. Its citizens are at once among the richest and the most economically insecure in the developed world. While income inequality was once on the decline, over the last twenty years the distribution of wealth and prosperity in the nation has become more unequal. Individuals and families at greatest risk for poverty are men with less than a college education, people of color (especially blacks and Hispanics), working families and families headed by women, and a significant number of the nation's elderly, who live at or close to the poverty line. A reflection on late 1950s America reveals a nation poised to embrace a vision of opportunity shared by all. It is a reflection we begin with to tell the story of America today. America is not the nation it envisioned itself being four decades ago. In the land of opportunity, many of its citizens experience poverty, economic insecurity, and income inequality on a daily basis.

The Demography of Poverty: Starting in the 1950s

In 1959, according to federal poverty statistics, at least 20.8% of families lived in poverty (Table 3). While 16.5% of white families lived below the poverty line, 54.9% of black families were poor. One out of two female-headed households lived below the poverty line. Two thirds of black female-headed households lived in poverty. More than one in four children lived below the poverty line in 1959 regardless of whether the family was headed by a male or female (Table 4). Rates were significantly higher for children of color compared with white children (39.6% versus 11.0%).

It was not until 1972 that the federal government published poverty statistics for Hispanic families. Hispanic families, too, had high rates of poverty—22.3% in the early 1970s. Almost one third of Hispanic children also were poor (Table 5).

Poverty status of families by race, percent, and numbers values, 1959			
Race	Total number in families	Number below poverty level	Percent
All	165,858	34,562	20.8%
White	47,802	24,443	16.5
Black	n/a	9,112	54.9

Numbers in thousands

Table 3. *One fifth of the nation was poor in the late 1950s*

Poverty status of children by family affiliation and race, 1959			
Race	Related children in families	Number below poverty level	Percent
All	63,995	17,208	26.9%
White	55,320	6,079	11.0
Black	9,384	3,716	39.6

Numbers in thousands

Table 4. *One out of four children were in poverty in 1959*

Poverty status of households and related children of Hispanic origin, 1972			
	Total number	Number below poverty level	Percent
Households	10,099	2,252	22.3%
Families with children	4,736	1,424	30.1

Numbers in thousands

Table 5. *Almost one third of Hispanic families with children were poor in 1972*

The Geography of Poverty

In the first half of the 20th century, poverty was primarily confined to rural areas. In 1959, while 18.3% of central city residents lived below the poverty line, 33.2% of nonmetro residents were classified as poor (Figure 9). Regional data show that in the 1960s, the poor were concentrated in the South—the location of 46% of the nation's poverty population (Map 4). The relatively unsettled West had the lowest poverty share (15%), followed by the Northeast (17%) and the Midwest (22%). Looking back to 1960, the poor were concentrated in Appalachia, the Mississippi Delta, the U.S.–Mexico border, Indian reservations, the Upper Peninsula, and the Atlantic Sea Coast (Map 5).

Poverty Forty Years Later: What Progress Has Been Made?

Despite a four-fold nominal increase in median family income over the last forty years, the absolute number of people in

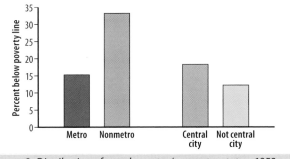

Figure 9. *Distribution of poor by metro/nonmetro status, 1959*

poverty has changed remarkably little in four decades (Figure 10). The lack of decline in the absolute number of persons in poverty is correlated with several factors. One that is clearly important is the stagnation of real median family incomes (1959 adjusted family income was $60,670 versus $43,318 in 2003).

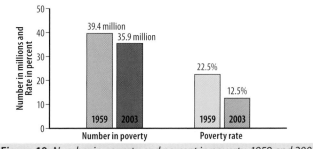

Figure 10. *Number in poverty and percent in poverty, 1959 and 2003*

Another distinct quality of poverty in the nation is its persistence. In 2003, as in 1959, a person of color was far more likely than a white person to be living below the poverty line. A person of color still had a one in four chance of being poor. For whites it was one in ten. Female-headed households had a one in three chance of living below the poverty line; for members of black female-headed households, the probability of living in poverty was even higher (38.9%). A child in America had almost a one in five chance of living in poverty (17.6% in 2003); a black child had a one in three chance of being poor (33.6%) (Table 6).

Percent of households by race, presence of children, and female-headed households, 2003				
Race	All people	Families	Age <18	Female-householder
All	12.5%	10.8%	17.6%	30.0%
White	10.5	8.7	13.4	25.6
Black	24.3	23.1	33.6	38.9
Hispanic	22.5	23.5	29.7	38.4

Numbers in percent below poverty line

Table 6. *Children and people of color are often poor*

Why Has the Poverty Rate Declined Since the 1960s?

In the last forty years, the largest positive change in poverty incidence occurred for the elderly: in 1959, 35.2% lived below the poverty line; today, that figure has dropped to 10%

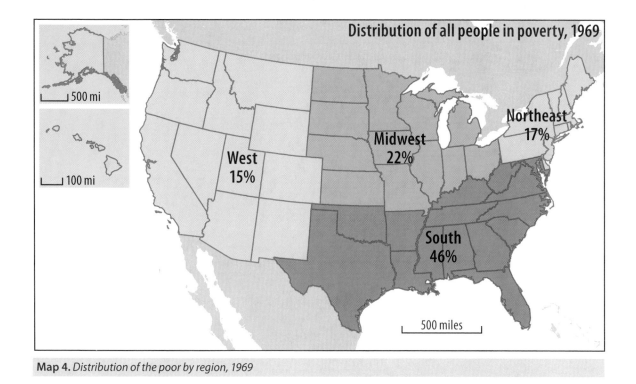

Map 4. *Distribution of the poor by region, 1969*

Distribution of all people in poverty, 1969

- Northeast 17%
- Midwest 22%
- West 15%
- South 46%

Percent of all people in poverty, 1960

2.2
20.9
34.4
43.7 — *all people average*
57.4
81.6

Map 5. *The geography of poverty in 1960*

(Table 7). All groups experienced a decline in poverty levels from the mid-1960s through the early 1970s. After that time, poverty rates stagnated and in some cases increased for population groups. Elderly poverty is the exception. Poverty rates for individuals over the age of 65 declined continuously over the last three decades of the 20th century. Since 2000, elderly poverty rates have begun to rise again, especially for women and people of color.

Race	Year	Total over 65 years	Number below poverty level	Percent
All	1959	15,557	5,481	35.2%
	2001	33,769	3,414	10.1
White	1959	n/a	4,744	33.1
	1974	19,206	2,460	12.8
	2001	29,790	2,656	8.9
Black	1965	n/a	711	62.5
	1974	1,721	591	34.3
	2001	2,853	626	21.9
Hispanic	1973	n/a	95	24.9
	2001	1,896	413	21.8

Numbers in thousands

Poverty status of individuals age 65+ by race and Hispanic origin, 1959–2001

Table 7. *Elderly have largely been lifted out of poverty*

Social Security has been one of the main reasons that more than half of the elderly over the age of 65 were able to remain out of poverty (Figure 11).

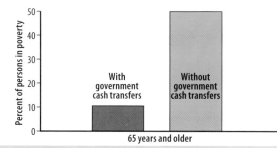

Figure 11. *Effect of Social Security benefits on poverty rates for the elderly, by age, 1995*

Still, more than 40% of elderly persons live on incomes only twice the national poverty level, which is approximately $18,000 a year.

Why Are People Poor?

People are poor because they have low incomes. Rising poverty is also linked to growing wealth inequality. The distribution of wealth (both net worth and type of wealth) has changed significantly through time. The top 5% of the population has increased its share of wealth between 1983 and 2001 to almost 58%. Financial wealth is held by very few people and the top 5% enjoy approximately 67.5% of total income (financial wealth equals the current value of all marketable or liquid assets less the current value of debts) (Table 8).

Comparisons of income shares tell a disquieting story. Measures of inequality such as the GINI coefficient indicate that current income distribution in the U.S. is substantially uneven. The nation is literally growing apart in the share of wealth and well-being, an issue we return to throughout this Atlas.

Distribution of wealth and income, 1983 and 2001

		Percentage share of the top income groups		
	Year	Top 1%	Next 4%	Top 20%
Net worth	1983	33.8%	22.3%	81.3%
	2001	33.4	25.8	84.4
Financial wealth	1983	42.9	25.1	91.3
	2001	39.7	27.8	91.3
Income	1982	12.8	13.3	51.9
	2000	20.0	15.2	58.6

Numbers in percent share of total income

Table 8. *The top 20% enjoy the majority of the nation's wealth*

Earned income (income earned over a calendar year) is also concentrated in the upper 5% of the population (35% of total). The top 20% of the population earns 58.6% of income.

Over the last twenty years, income inequality has grown. If we divide the U.S. population into five equal-sized groups based on their income (quintiles), we find that changes in income from 1977–2003 have brought the most benefits to the top quintile (Table 9). In 1977, the lowest 40% of families received 17% of income. The upper 20% of families received approximately 44% of total household income. By 2003, the lowest 40% of the population received only 12.5% of total family income while the top 20% received 50% of total family income.

Income distribution and measure of inequality in the U.S., 1977, 2002, and 2003

Income quintile	1977	2002	2003
Lowest	5.7%	3.5%	3.4%
Mid-low	11.5	8.5	8.7
Middle	16.4	13.8	14.8
Mid-high	22.8	23.3	23.4
High	44.2	49.7	49.8
GINI coefficient	–	0.462	0.464

Numbers in percent of total income

Table 9. *The wealthy enjoy the majority of the nation's earned income*

LIVED EXPERIENCES

children • women • black families • black male incarceration • Hispanics • elderly • working poor • wealthy families

Children: Poverty in America Starts with Children

In 2001, twelve million children under the age of 18 lived in poverty in the United States (Figure 12).

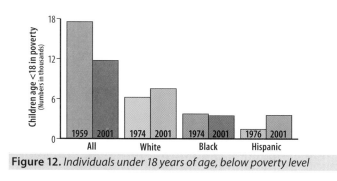

Figure 12. *Individuals under 18 years of age, below poverty level*

The Demographics of Poverty

Although children of color are more likely to live in poverty, the largest number of poor children are non-Hispanic white and their numbers are growing. Almost eight million white children live below the poverty line. The youngest children are at most risk. 18.2% of children under the age of 5 lives below the poverty level. One in six of all children lives in poverty today (Table 10).

Children in poverty as a percent of all children by age, 1999

Age group	Percent of age group in poverty
<5	18.2
5	17.6
6–11	16.9
12–17	14.8
<17	16.6

Table 10. *Very young children are susceptible to living in poverty*

The Geography of Poverty

The geography of poverty is stark. States with very high child poverty rates are predominantly in the South (Map 6). Thirty-one percent of children in the nation's capitol live in poverty. In eight states (Alabama, Arizona, Arkansas, District of Columbia, Louisiana, Mississippi, New Mexico, Tennessee, and West Virginia), at least one in four children is poor (Table 11).

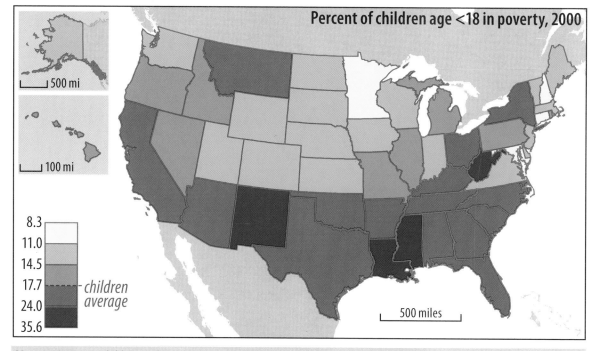

Percent of children age <18 in poverty, 2000

8.3	
11.0	
14.5	
17.7	*children average*
24.0	
35.6	

Map 6. *Most poor children under 18 live in the South and Southwest*

Child poverty rate by state, top and bottom ten, 2003

Rank:	Top ten		Rank:	Bottom ten	
1	New Hampshire	8.6%	51	Wash. D.C.	31.0%
2	Colorado	11.0	50	Arkansas	31.2
	Hawaii	11.0	49	Louisiana	30.8
4	New Jersey	11.4	48	West Virginia	30.5
5	Minnesota	11.5	47	Mississippi	28.8
6	Connecticut	11.9	46	New Mexico	27.4
7	Maine	13.9	45	Alabama	25.6
8	Nebraska	14.0	43	Arizona	25.0
9	Nevada	14.6		Tennessee	25.0
	Virginia	14.6	42	Oklahoma	24.8

Table 11. *Stark differences in where poor children live*

Declining Protections: The Absence of Basic Needs

For children, being poor often means lacking access to basic needs, such as food, clothing, shelter, and health care. One in seven children in the United States does not have health care. Almost 25% of children in Texas and New Mexico are not covered by health care (Map 7). Children living in poverty are more likely to lack required childhood vaccinations compared with non-poor children (Figure 13). Twenty-five percent of children do not receive recommended preventive health care visits and immunizations. Children of color and children who live in central cities are more likely to lack needed vaccinations.

Changes in public policies in support of poor families have increased the vulnerability of poor children. Lack of access to health care, decent affordable housing, and income supports contribute to early childhood economic insecurity. Public as-

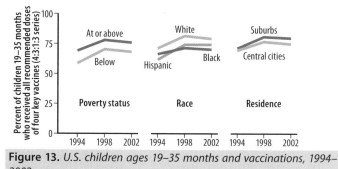

Figure 13. *U.S. children ages 19–35 months and vaccinations, 1994–2002*

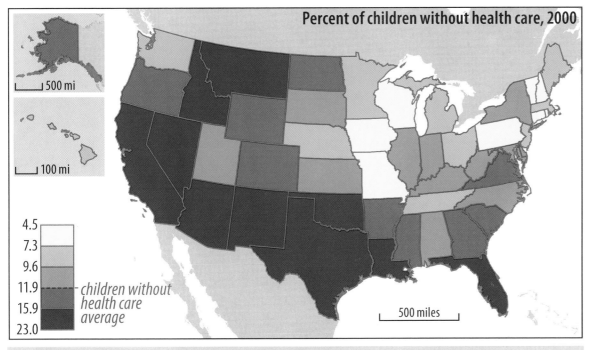

Percent of children without health care, 2000

500 mi
100 mi

4.5
7.3
9.6
11.9
15.9
23.0

*children without
health care
average*

Map 7. *Percent of children without health care high in the Southwest*

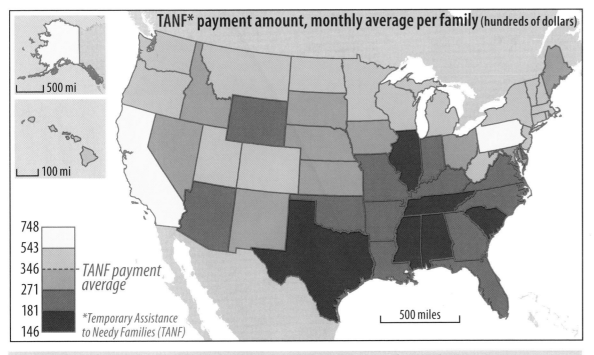

TANF* payment amount, monthly average per family (hundreds of dollars)

500 mi
100 mi

748
543
346
271
181
146

*TANF payment
average*

**Temporary Assistance
to Needy Families (TANF)*

Map 8. *Temporary Assistance to Needy Families (TANF) benefits for a three-person family, July 2001*

sistance is becoming increasingly unavailable and no state provides assistance at a level that raises a family of three above the poverty line (Map 8).

Child Poverty Linked to Work that Fails to Pay a Living Wage

The lack of health care is symptomatic of a larger challenge of childhood in America. Poor children largely come from low-wage working families. Seventy-one percent of poor children are members of families who work but do not make a living wage. These families are predominantly headed by two parents of working age.

Geography of the Working Poor

Low-wage working families are found throughout the nation. States in the Northeast have relatively low levels of working poor, whereas in more than 30 states over 30% of their families are working but poor (Map 9). In some states, the percent of all children who live in low-income working families is as high as 49% (Map 10). Working and being poor in America is increasingly linked to an abundance of jobs that require limited education. Over the last twenty years, the nation has experienced job growth in occupations where investments in education yield little or no increase in wages. And yet, in 42% of families who are working but poor, at least one parent has some postsecondary education.

Government Provides Little Help

Over the last decade, the level of federal funding for children in America has declined despite the fact that children have become more vulnerable and have access to fewer sources of government support. Federal funds in support of healthy children also have changed. Today, the majority of funding for children is in the form of tax credits and interest subsidies to parents. Overall, while expenditures on domestic programs in 1997 increased from 9 to 16% since 1960, little of this growth has benefited children. By far the largest beneficiaries of changes in government spending are the nation's elderly.

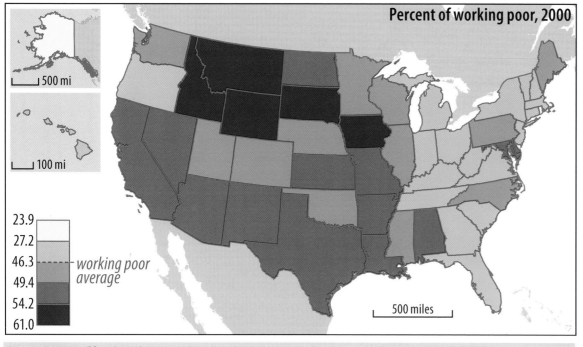

Percent of working poor, 2000

500 mi

100 mi

23.9
27.2
46.3 —— *working poor average*
49.4
54.2
61.0

500 miles

Map 9. *Percent of families who are working but poor*

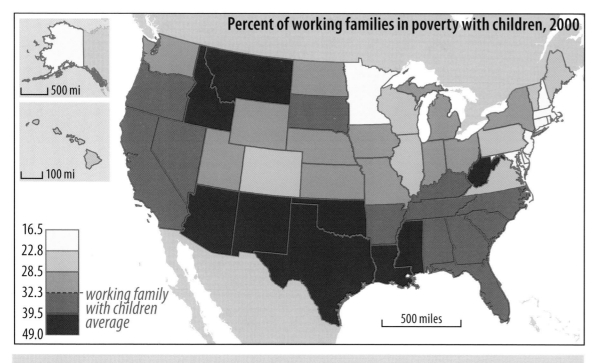

Percent of working families in poverty with children, 2000

500 mi

100 mi

16.5
22.8
28.5
32.3 —— *working family with children average*
39.5
49.0

500 miles

Map 10. *Percent of working families in poverty with children*

The Future

Education is critical to getting out of poverty. Over the last thirty years, real wages for workers with less than a high school education have declined by 19% while real wages for persons with some college have increased by 16%. The lack of a high school education typically relegates America's children to a life of low earnings and potential future economic instability. Despite the clear link between education and prosperity, school drop-out rates are high by international standards.

Disparities in the completion rates of America's high school students are disquieting. Graduation rates in schools with predominantly minority populations lag by almost 18 percentage points behind majority white districts. Similar gaps are evident in poor districts, districts with high proportions of students who lack proficiency in English, and districts with a high percentage of students in special education programs. Evidence demonstrates that students of color are severely disadvantaged by both location and income profile.

There are striking regional differences as well. In general, drop-out rates are highest in the West and the South (Map 11). At the same time, there are significant differences within regions based on race and income characteristics of the student population. For example, schools in the Northeast whose population is predominantly white, graduate students at a higher rate than schools with predominantly minority populations. Students attending schools in central city districts also exhibit correspondingly lower rates of completion compared with suburban and rural districts. In 2000, high school-age students in the lowest 20% of family income groups were six times as likely as their peers from families in the top 20% of the income distribution to drop out of high school (10% vs. 2%). Children of color are far more likely to leave high school before completion compared with white children (Figure 14).

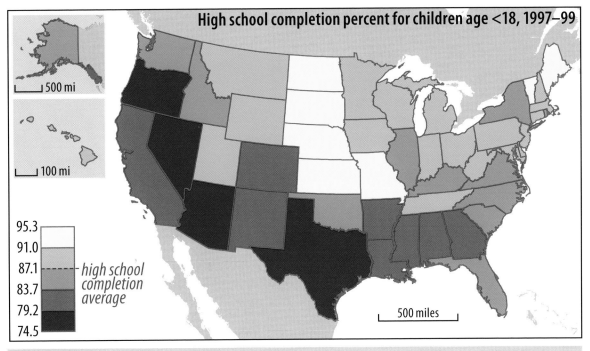

Map 11. *High school completion rates are low in the West*

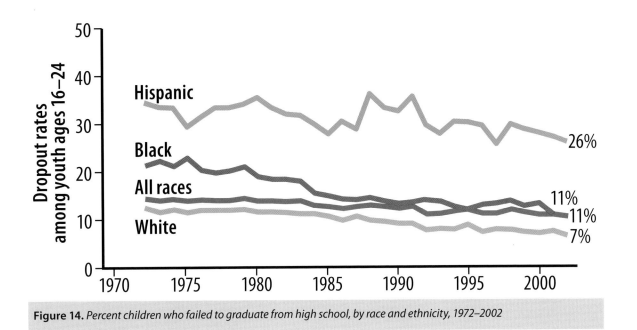

Figure 14. *Percent children who failed to graduate from high school, by race and ethnicity, 1972–2002*

Women: *Often Poor, Vulnerable, and Lacking Access to Basic Needs*

The story of women in America today reflects many of the concerns commonly highlighted in research on the persistence of poverty: higher numbers in poverty compared to men, greater vulnerability to the condition, and lower access to the basic needs that keep their families together.

Women in America face many challenges. The majority of poor females are white women (approximately 13 million in 2001). However, women of color are more likely than white women to be poor (Table 12). Women are more likely to live in poverty than men. They also are more likely to live in poverty as they age (Table 13). In the absence of Social Security, elderly women are more likely to live in poverty than men (Figure 15). Social Security payments are vital in keeping elderly women out of poverty (Figure 16).

Percent in poverty, females by race, 2001

Race	Percent below poverty level
All	12.5%
White	13.7
Black	26.5
Hispanic	24.4

Table 12. *Women of color are poorer than the general population*

Percent in poverty, males and females by age, 2001

	Percent below poverty level	
Age	Male	Female
<18	17.7%	17.6%
65+	7.3	12.5
75+	7.5	14.3

Table 13. *Women are more likely to be poor than men as they age*

Figure 15. *Poverty rates: Elderly women by marital status*

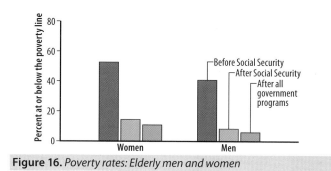

Figure 16. *Poverty rates: Elderly men and women*

Low pay for women in the workforce almost requires them to work multiple jobs to make ends meet. Almost 50% of all multiple jobholders in 2002 were women. This figure has significantly increased since the 1970s (Figure 17). In 2002, the rate of women holding multiple jobs was higher than that for men (Figure 18).

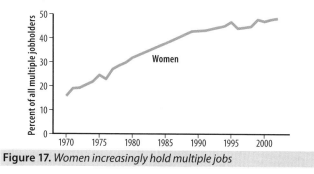

Figure 17. *Women increasingly hold multiple jobs*

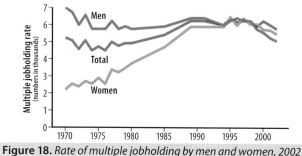

Figure 18. *Rate of multiple jobholding by men and women, 2002*

Why Are Women Poor?: The Work Connection

Women's poverty is directly related to their experience in the labor force, differences in male versus female earnings, the jobs women have access to, and wage discrimination. Despite the fact that women are completing college at a rate higher than men, their wages do not reflect this.

Women's paid labor continues to fall short of men's compensation rates for the same job. Women earn 76¢ on the dollar for every dollar earned by a man. Reductions in the wage gap over the last decade are not primarily due to rising wages overall, but to a stagnation in male wages (Figure 19).

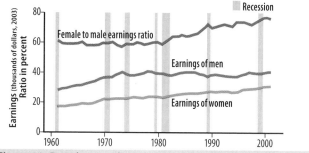

Figure 19. *Female-to-male earnings ratio and median earnings of full-time, year-round workers 15 years old and over, by sex, 1960–2003*

The biggest pay gap is between white women and men. Women of color earn lower median incomes than white women (Figure 20). Female-headed households with a family (both white and black) earn significantly lower incomes compared with males both with and without families (Figure 21). Female households without a family are even worse off, earning just 34% of a married couple's income level.

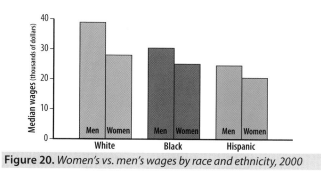

Figure 20. *Women's vs. men's wages by race and ethnicity, 2000*

Numerous factors contribute to the enduring wage gap between men and women. While discrimination is a primary cause, occupational segregation and differences in remuneration rates for comparable levels of education also contribute to the differences (Figure 22).

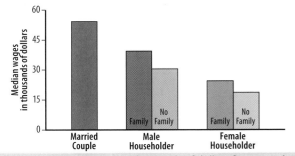

Figure 21. *Median wages in thousands of dollars for married couples, and male and female households with and without families, 2003*

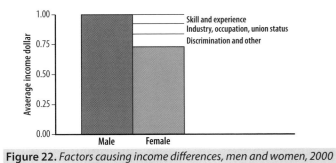

Figure 22. *Factors causing income differences, men and women, 2000*

Occupational segregation is a significant determinant of the male-female wage gap. Women primarily find employment in service and clerical occupations (Figure 23). In technical occupations women receive higher wages than women in the service sector; nonetheless, the wage gap between men and women is greater in more technical occupations (Table 14).

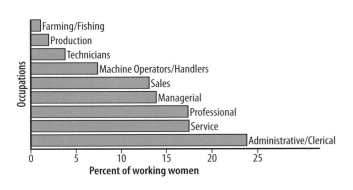

Figure 23. *Gender distribution in occupations, 2000*

Weekly earnings by sex and occupation, 2000				
Occupation	Women's weekly earnings	Men's weekly earnings	Earnings ratio	Women's annual loss
Administrative/Clerical	$427	$539	0.79	$5,824
Service	304	402	0.75	5,096
Professional	707	939	0.75	12,064
Managerial	652	967	0.67	16,380
Sales	399	666	0.60	13,884
Machine operators/Handlers	337	472	0.71	7,020
Technicians	431	626	0.69	10,140
Production	428	606	0.71	9,256
Farming/Fishing	283	341	0.83	3,016

Table 14. *Income inequality is most evident in higher skilled jobs*

Today, women are more likely to go to and graduate from college than are men. They are becoming a more important component of the educated labor force through time. Despite this development, women with the same level of education continue to earn less than men. Even with a Ph.D., a woman is

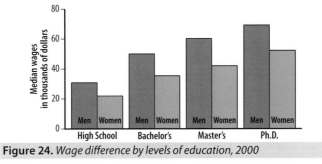

Figure 24. *Wage difference by levels of education, 2000*

likely to earn only $1,000 more than a man with a Bachelor's degree (Figure 24).

The Geography of Poverty

While poor women are dispersed throughout the nation, there are obvious patterns based on race and regional industrial structure (Maps 12–15). Poor black women are more likely to be found in Appalachia and the Mississippi Delta. Poor white women are found in Appalachia, the mid South, and the Great Plains. Latinas are found predominantly in major industrial states, including Pennsylvania and New York. For elderly women, conditions are even more stark. Elderly women in the Midwest are more likely to live in poverty than women living in other regions of the nation.

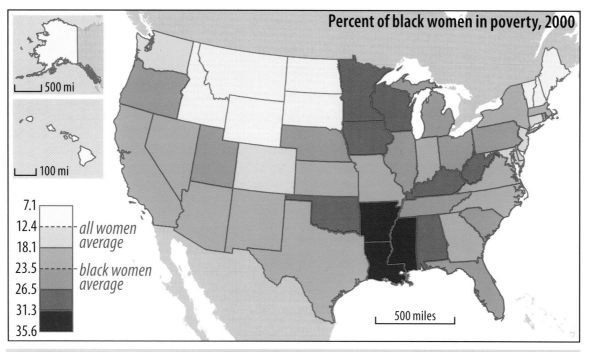

Map 12. *Poor black women are concentrated in the South and the Upper Midwest*

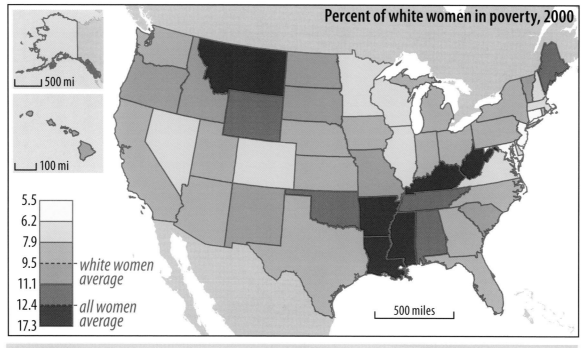

Map 13. *White women in poverty tend to live in the South and West*

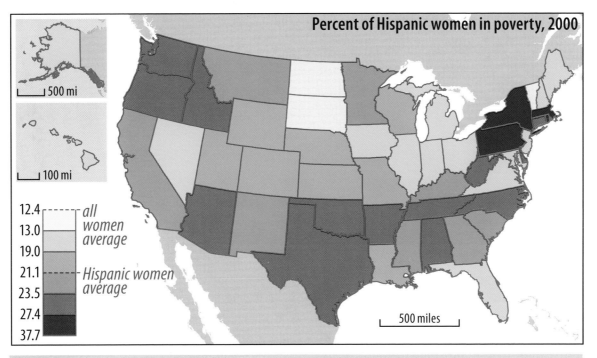

Map 14. *Poor Hispanic women are concentrated in the West*

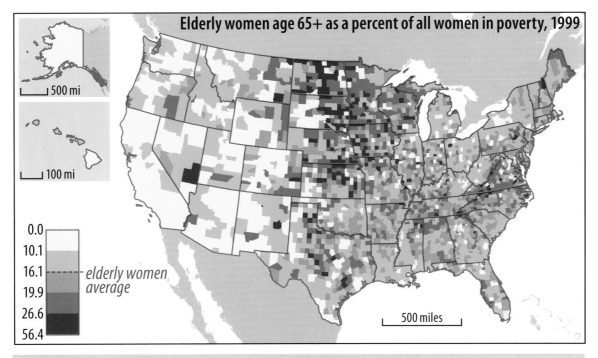

Map 15. *Elderly women in the Midwest have high poverty rates*

Black Families at Risk

Another glaring paradox in America is the fact that the nation has a significant black middle class (based on family income levels of $40,000 or more) and yet the number of families below the poverty line and the number of black children living in extreme poverty has increased since the mid-1990s (Figure 25). Despite being employed, black families and children still find it hard to get by.

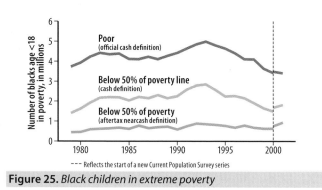

Figure 25. *Black children in extreme poverty*

The Demographics of Poverty

In America, blacks are almost three times as likely to live in poverty as whites. Almost one million black children live in extreme poverty. Children living in a household headed by a single parent have especially high rates of poverty. Thirty-six percent of children living in a female-headed household live in poverty (Table 15).

Poverty status of black households by sex and type of family, 2002 and 2003						
	Male householder, no wife present			Female householder, no husband present		
Year	Total	Number	Percent	Total	Number	Percent
2003	804	194	24.1%	4068	1496	36.8%
2002	793	165	20.8%	4072	1454	35.7%

Numbers in thousands

Table 15. *Single-parent household poverty is worse for women*

Why Are Blacks More Likely to be Poor than Whites?

The origins and persistence of black poverty are complex, but ultimately tied to enduring racism and social exclusion

as found in labor market and housing conditions, and lead to job and occupational discrimination, limited access to quality education, and spatial segregation in the housing market. For many blacks, especially men, work often doesn't pay a living wage. Young black men are twice as likely to be working poor as white men; the same is true for black women (Table 16).

Working but poor by race, sex, and age, 2000				
Sex	Age	Total	White	Black
Total	16+	4.9%	4.3%	9.6%
	16–19	10.4	8.8	23.3
	20–24	9.9	8.8	17.1
Men	16+	4.4	4.1	7.1
	16–19	9.4	8.0	20.2
	20–24	7.9	7.3	11.1
Women	16+	5.5	4.5	11.8
	16–19	11.6	9.5	26.5
	20–24	12.1	10.4	22.3

Numbers in percent

Table 16. *Women and blacks are most likely to be working and poor*

Employment and Wage Levels Affect Family Income

For all black males, regardless of age, labor force participation rates are lower than those for white males; black males are far more likely to be unemployed than white males (Figure 26).

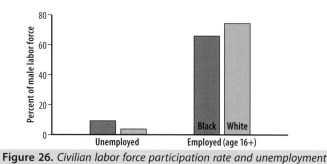

Figure 26. *Civilian labor force participation rate and unemployment rate by sex and race, 1999*

Wages for black men are lower than for their white male counterparts. This is true even holding education levels constant (Table 17). The effect on family incomes is significant. The average income of black families is substantially lower than that of white families. The median and mean incomes for white

Annual income of people age 25+, by educational attainment, sex, and race, 1997						
	Total	Less than 9th grade	9th–12th grade, no diploma	High school graduate	Some college or associate degree	Bachelor's degree or more
White male	$31,497	$12,849	$18,335	$26,658	$32,258	$49,648
White female	16,133	7,946	9,068	13,414	18,166	29,707
Black male	21,210	9,320	12,803	20,844	26,263	35,563
Black female	15,348	6,950	8,192	14,222	20,171	30,825

Table 17. *Equal education does not yield equal income for blacks*

families are $40,000 and $54,000 versus $25,000 and $34,000 for black families.

Access to Income and Wealth Differs by Race

In America, income and wealth are highly skewed based on race. Black families' income and wealth are half that of white families (Table 18). Since 1982, this ratio of black to white income levels has actually declined, as has net worth share. While the financial assets of blacks have increased over time,

Family income and wealth for whites and blacks, 1983–2001					
		Means		Medians	
Income/Wealth	Year	White	Black	White	Black
Income	1982	$ 55.4	$29.8	$ 39.0	$21.7
	2000	75.9	36.8	44.0	25.0
Net worth	1983	259.9	50.8	77.7	5.2
	2001	465.8	66.3	106.4	10.7
Financial wealth	1983	198.9	25.6	21.6	0.0
	2001	369.7	43.2	42.1	1.1
Homeownership rate	1983	68.1	44.3		
	2001	74.1	47.4		
Percent of households with zero or negative net worth	1983	11.3	34.1		
	2001	13.1	30.9		

Numbers in thousands of dollars

Table 18. *Income, net worth and wealth much higher for whites*

they are still only slightly more than one tenth those of whites. Black families are about half as likely to own a home as white families; more than 30% of black families have a negative net worth compared with only 13% of white families.

Geography of Black Family Poverty

Black families living in poverty are found throughout the U.S., with the highest concentrations of black families in poverty in the South and Midwest (Map 16).

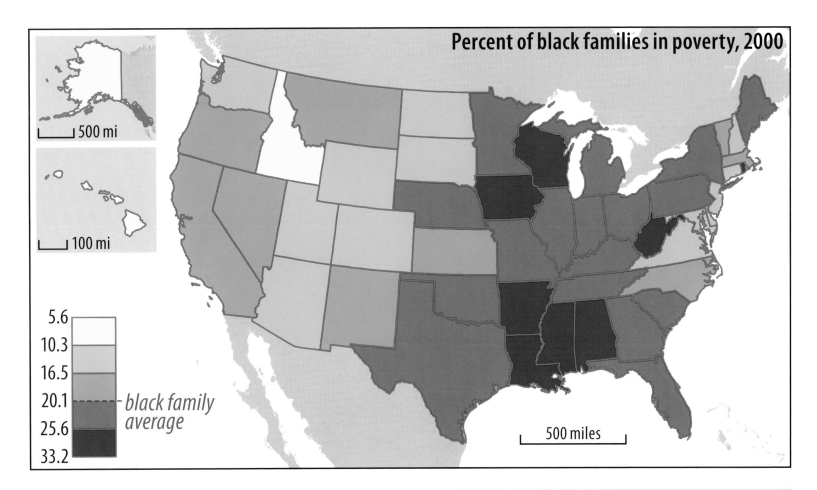

Percent of black families in poverty, 2000

500 mi

100 mi

5.6
10.3
16.5
20.1 — — black family
25.6   average
33.2

500 miles

Map 16. *Percent of black families in poverty, 2000*

Black Male Incarceration: *Impacts on the Family*

Twenty years ago, black men and families were on track in terms of marriage rates, college attendance, and access to jobs that paid living wages. This fact provided some hope that our nation would unite without differences based on race. Over the last twenty years, however, much of that dream has been dashed as living-wage jobs have fallen out of the reach of a growing number of blacks.

The challenges facing black families have worsened over the last twenty years. In 1950, more than 78% of all black families were two-parent. By 1990, this number had decreased to only slightly more than 50% (Figure 27). Three factors—economic instability, incarceration, and mortality—are significant factors in the dissolution of the black family. What explains this dramatic turn of events? Lack of work, work that doesn't pay a living wage, and outright poverty discourage family formation and erode family stability.

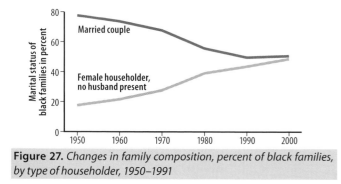

Figure 27. *Changes in family composition, percent of black families, by type of householder, 1950–1991*

In 2000, black men were more likely to be behind bars than in college. A total of 791,600 black men were in jail or prison and 603,032 were enrolled in colleges or universities. This figure changed markedly since 1980, when only 143,000 black men were in jail compared to 463,700 enrolled in colleges or universities. According to federal statistics, between 1980 and 2000 three times as many black men were added to the prison system as were added to the nation's colleges and universities.

The costs of incarceration are exceptionally high for black men: in most states felons lose their right to vote after serving time in prison. Thirteen percent of the black adult male population has lost the right to vote due to involvement with the criminal justice system. In many states blacks, predominantly men, are disenfranchised (Map 17).

There has been an unprecedented rise in the number of black males incarcerated over the last decade, leading to their disproportionate representation in the U.S. criminal justice system. Although blacks comprise only 13% of the population, they total 30% of persons arrested, 41% of persons jailed, and 49% of persons in prison. Nine percent of black men are in jail compared to 2% of white adults. One in three black men between the ages of 20 and 29 has served time in some type of correctional institution. One in ten black men in their 20s and early 30s is currently in jail. Given the rate of incarceration experienced by black males, a black man ages 25–40 has a one in three chance of being incarcerated during his most productive wage-earning years (Figure 28).

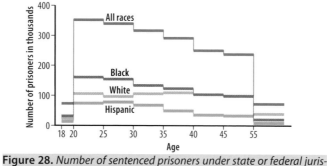

Figure 28. *Number of sentenced prisoners under state or federal jurisdiction, by race, Hispanic origin, and age, 2002*

Black males make up a disproportionate number of sentenced prisoners under state and federal jurisdiction. Comprising 5.9% of the total population, they represent 45% of sentenced prisoners. A black male, especially between the ages of 25–29, is nine times more likely to be incarcerated as a white male of similar age (Figure 29).

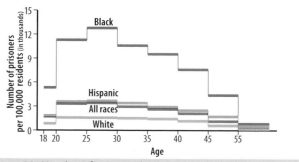

Figure 29. *Number of sentenced prisoners under state or federal jurisdiction per 100,000 residents, race, Hispanic origin, and age, 2002*

The spatial distribution of incarceration rates of African Americans in jails and prisons varies considerably across the nation. A black male in Washington, DC is 28 times more likely to be arrested than a white person. In addition, there appears to be a regional bias in the probability of being incarcerated in a jail or in a prison, with higher probabilities found in larger northern, midwestern, and Plains states (Map 18).

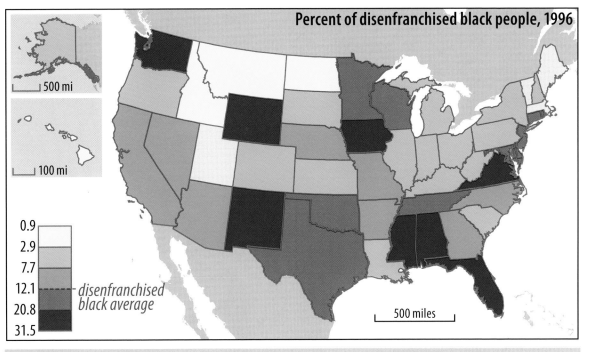

Percent of disenfranchised black people, 1996

500 mi

100 mi

0.9
2.9
7.7
12.1 -- *disenfranchised black average*
20.8
31.5

500 miles

Map 17. *Disenfranchised blacks, 1996*

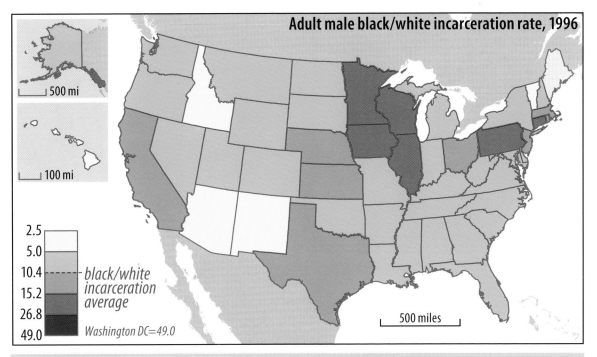

Adult male black/white incarceration rate, 1996

500 mi

100 mi

2.5
5.0
10.4 -- *black/white incarceration average*
15.2
26.8
49.0 *Washington DC=49.0*

500 miles

Map 18. *The black/white incarceration ratio in the nation's capitol far exceeds the average*

Hard Work and Low Pay Define the Lives of Hispanic Americans

In 2005 Hispanics became the largest minority group in the nation (13% of the total population), accounting for more than 35 million people. Over the 1990s, the Hispanic population increased by 10 million people and accounted for almost 40% of the nation's population growth (38%). According to some estimates, by the middle of the 21st century Hispanics will account for 25% of the population (Table 19).

County type	Counties	Population, 2000	Change in population, 1990–2000	Population, 2000	Change in population, 1990–2000
Nonmetro counties	2,289	3,175,953	67%	52,983,373	8%
High-growth Hispanic	149	526,942	345	7,254,164	15
Established Hispanic	230	1,602,630	32	2,931,071	9
All other	1913	1,046,381	84	42,798,138	7
Metro counties	813	32,129,864	57	193,132,712	9

During the 1990s, nonmetro and metro Hispanic populations grew far more rapidly

Table 19. *The population of Hispanics grew rapidly over the 1990s*

Our understanding of the historical geography of Hispanics in America is obscured to some degree by the changing definition of "Hispanic" used by the census. Prior to 1980 ambiguities in the census definition of "Hispanic or Latino in origin" reduced the precision with which individuals of Hispanic origin were enumerated. The Spanish origin population in 1970 was overstated in some states, especially in the Midwest and South, because some respondents interpreted the questionnaire category of "Central or South American" to mean central or southern United States. Interpretation of the 1970 data should take this issue into consideration in the data presented in this section.

The Geography of Hispanic Americans

During the 1990s, Hispanics not only grew in share of the national population, but also began to disperse spatially across the nation. Whereas in the 1970s Hispanics were concentrated in fewer than ten states, by 2000 people of Hispanic origin were found in increasing numbers in regions of the country where manufacturing and agricultural industries were concentrated (Maps 19, 20).

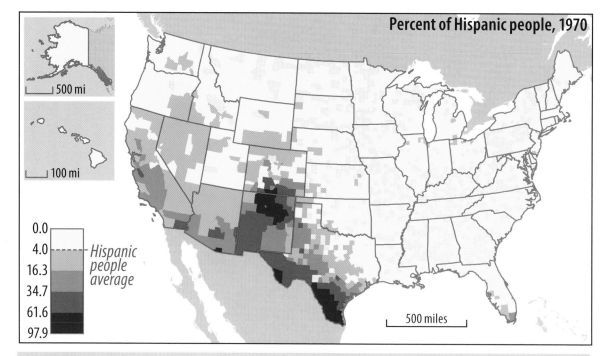

Map 19. *Percent Hispanics in counties in the U.S., 1970*

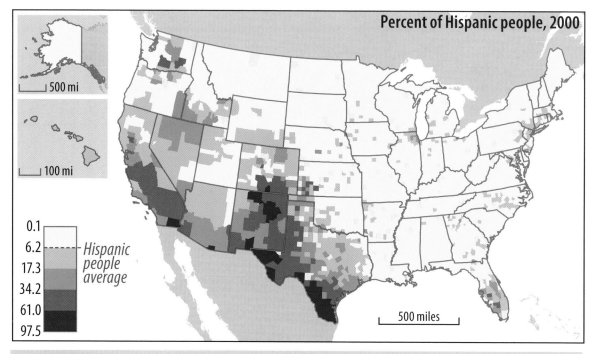

Map 20. *Percent Hispanics in counties in the U.S., 2000*

Working Hard Yields Low Returns for Hispanic Americans

For the entire 20th century, the United States has benefited enormously from persons of Hispanic origin. Since the Second World War, Hispanics have been recruited deliberately to fill the ranks of working persons. One of the key recruiting programs was the Bracero program, which originated from a treaty signed between the U.S. and Mexico. The program was designed to allow the recruitment and employment of Mexican citizens to reduce labor shortages in agriculture and other labor-intensive industries. Although the program formally ended in the 1960s, Mexican Americans have and continue to occupy a central place in the American labor market. Hispanics have high rates of labor force participation compared with other groups in the population (Table 20).

The U.S. labor force: A racial and ethnic breakdown		Non-Hispanic		
	Hispanic	White	Black	Other
Labor force participation rate	69.1%	66.3%	64.9%	66.0%

Table 20. *Percent labor force participation by Hispanics compared to other population groups in the U.S.*

Hispanics' positions in the labor market are characterized by low prestige and low wages (Figures 30 and 31). Whereas 31.4% of the overall male population works in managerial and professional occupations, only 14.6% of Hispanic males work in comparable occupations. Hispanic males are more likely to find employment in farming, construction, and production jobs than non-Hispanic males.

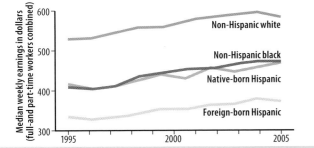

Figure 30. *Median weekly earnings by race and ethnicity: Median weekly earnings of Hispanics are two-thirds of those for non-Hispanic whites*

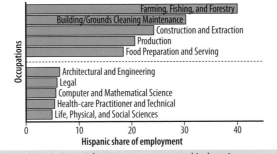
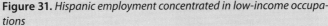

Figure 31. *Hispanic employment concentrated in low-income occupations*

Poverty rates in the Latino community are significantly higher than the population as a whole (Figure 32).

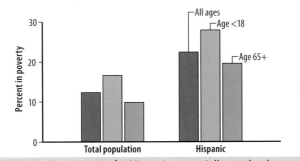

Figure 32. *Poverty rates for Hispanics, especially youth, almost twice the national average, 1999*

Poverty rates are especially high for Hispanic children. Child poverty rates are approximately 10 percentage points above the national average for all children (27.8% versus 16.6%). At the same time, elderly Hispanics are twice as likely to live in poverty compared with the general elderly population.

The Geography of Hispanic Poverty

The spatial distribution of Hispanic poverty mirrors the distribution of the Hispanic population. Hispanics face a high probability of being poor due to limited access to high-paying jobs and low levels of assets in Hispanic families (Maps 21–24).

Despite high rates of labor force participation by both men and women and members of families with children, Hispanics enjoy levels of wealth only one-tenth those of white households. The recession of the 1990s hit Hispanic households particularly hard. On average, they lost 25% of their wealth compared with white families (Figure 33).

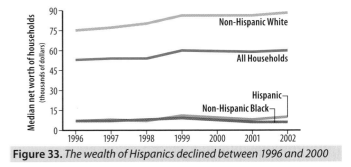

Figure 33. *The wealth of Hispanics declined between 1996 and 2000*

Despite high rates of labor force participation, Hispanic families have experienced only limited growth in well being. Migration has done little to improve the conditions of Hispanic families. Lack of labor market mobility and access to limited and often poor-quality education significantly hamper the economic mobility of Hispanic Americans (Maps 25–26).

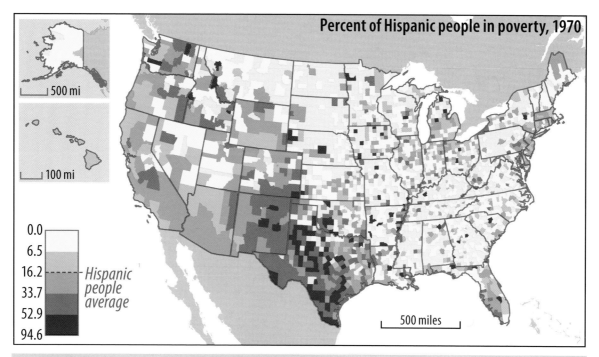

Percent of Hispanic people in poverty, 1970

0.0	
6.5	
16.2	Hispanic
33.7	people
52.9	average
94.6	

Map 21. *Hispanic poverty concentrated in the Southwest, 1970*

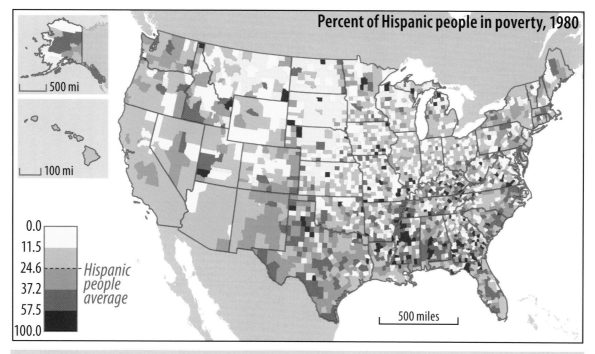

Percent of Hispanic people in poverty, 1980

0.0	
11.5	
24.6	Hispanic
37.2	people
57.5	average
100.0	

Map 22. *Hispanic poverty begins to spread out into the industrial heartland, the 1980s*

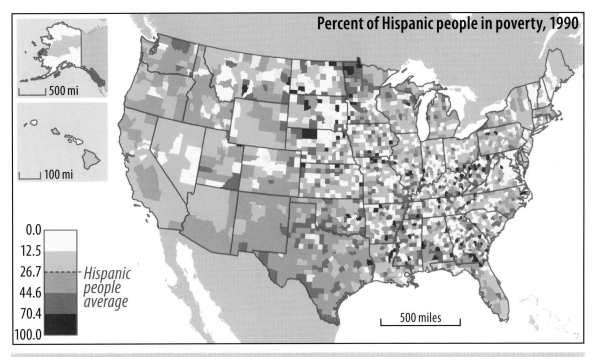

Map 23. *By the 1990s, Hispanic poverty evident in the Northeast*

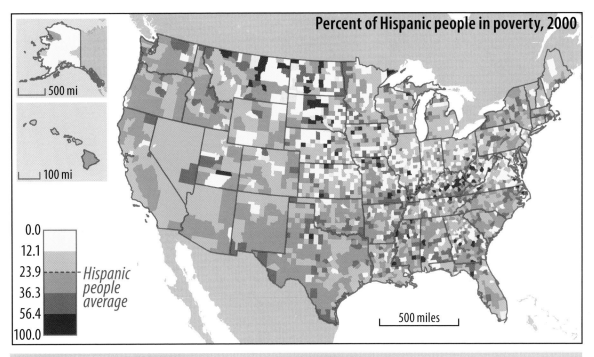

Map 24. *In 2000, Hispanic poverty rates above the average in most industrial areas*

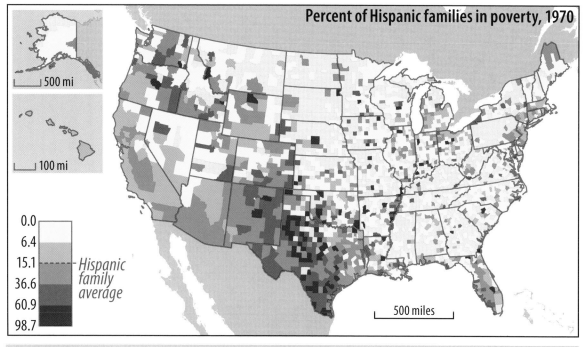

Percent of Hispanic families in poverty, 1970

500 mi

100 mi

0.0
6.4
15.1 --- *Hispanic family average*
36.6
60.9
98.7

500 miles

Map 25. *Hispanic families were poor even in the industrial heartland, 1970*

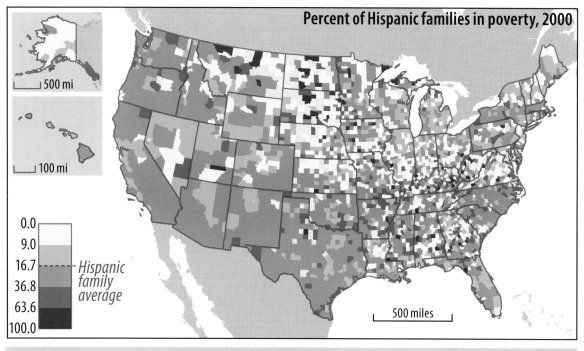

Percent of Hispanic families in poverty, 2000

500 mi

100 mi

0.0
9.0
16.7 --- *Hispanic family average*
36.8
63.6
100.0

500 miles

Map 26. *By 2000, family poverty among Hispanics is high in the Southwest*

Elderly: Social Programs Keep Many Out of Poverty

In 1959, poverty among the elderly was greater than 30% (Figure 34). By providing indexed income and medical care through Social Security, Medicare, and Medicaid, the poverty rate among Americans over the age of 65 declined to 10% in 2003. More than any single effort, Social Security has meant some measure of economic security for millions of American elderly (Photo 1).

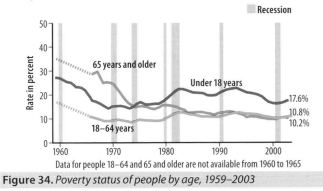

Figure 34. *Poverty status of people by age, 1959–2003*

Photo 1. *Vintage image from the birth of the Social Security Act*

The importance of Social Security as a means of lifting elderly Americans out of poverty is all the more momentous today as the United States increasingly becomes a society of older individuals. By 2030, it is projected that one third of the population will be over the age of 65. Americans are living longer now than ever before (Figure 35).

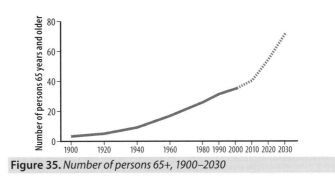

Figure 35. *Number of persons 65+, 1900–2030*

Social Security Lifts Many Out of Poverty

In 2001, Social Security payouts represented the largest share of income for the elderly—39% according to census data. Social Security is an essential source of income, especially for individuals in the lower income group of elderly Americans (Figure 36). Without Social Security, nearly half (47.6%) of Americans aged 65 or over would have been poor in 1995 (Figure 37).

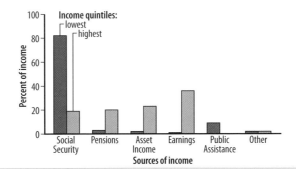

Figure 36. *Shares of aggregate income for the lowest and highest income quintiles, by source, 2001*

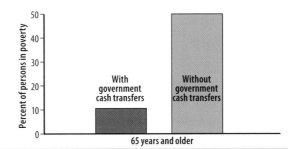

Figure 37. *Effect of Social Security benefits on poverty rates for older population by age, 1995*

The disparities across the elderly population in terms of levels and sources of income are telling. The median household income of individuals over the age of 65 is $33,802, including all forms of income (e.g., pensions and investment income) whereas the median income earned from employment is only $14,251. For individuals living off earned income only, and those who are either ineligible to earn Social Security or earn too little on Social Security and must therefore work, their level of economic security is substantially lower than that in households that have retirement income from pensions, investments, and other sources of wealth.

The Demography of Elderly Poverty

Despite the great progress made in establishing a level of economic security for the elderly, poverty still does exist for older Americans and it is unevenly distributed across the population. Elderly women 65 years and older were more likely to be poor than elderly men in 2002. At age 75, women are almost twice as likely to live in poverty as men (Table 21). Unmarried women and elderly persons of color are nearly twice as likely to be poor or nearly poor than men and married couples (Figure 38). Seventeen percent of elderly African American men and 27% of elderly African American women live below the poverty line (Figure 39). Among elderly Hispanics, 20% of men and 24% of women were poor (Figure 40). Without Social Security benefits, 54.5% of older Hispanics would live below the poverty threshold.

Percent in poverty by residence, sex, and age, 2001				
	Metro	Central city	Suburbs	Nonmetro
Male 65+	6.3	9.5	4.7	9.3
Male 75+	6.7	10.0	5.0	9.1
Female 65+	11.8	14.9	10.0	14.4
Female 75+	12.5	15.5	10.9	17.1

Table 21. *The elderly poor live in central cities and nonmetro areas*

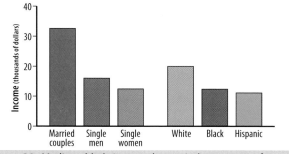

Figure 38. *Median elderly income, by marital status, sex of unmarried persons, race, and Hispanic origin, 2001*

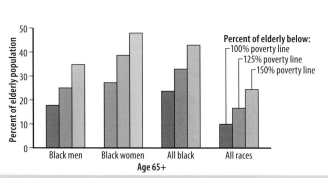

Figure 39. *Percent of blacks age 65 and older below or near poverty threshold in 2002*

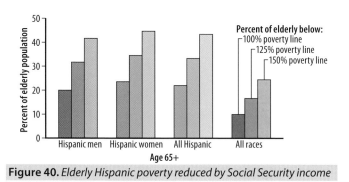

Figure 40. *Elderly Hispanic poverty reduced by Social Security income*

Poverty Rate Fails to Capture the True Cost of Living

According to the National Academies of Science, the current poverty measure, based solely on income, understates the income needs of the elderly. Two experimental measures that incorporate all sources of income minus the cost of living plus additional expenses associated with health care indicate the effective poverty rate for the elderly is much higher than that based purely on the income measure alone (Figure 41). According to the two alternative measures, elderly poverty is almost 50% higher than the overall national average.

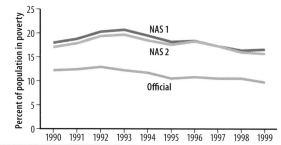

Figure 41. *Poverty rates using official and experimental measures for persons 65 and over, 1990–1999*

Geography of Poverty

The geographic location of the elderly in poverty varies considerably across states and rural and metro areas (Table 19). The poor and elderly tend to live in the South and in either the inner city or rural areas. Texas and Mississippi have some of the highest rates of elderly poverty in the nation (Map 27).

The geography of elderly poverty varies by gender. The percent of poor elderly women is particularly high in states in the Great Plains (Map 28).

While great strides have been made in providing economic security for America's elderly, there remains a fine line between security and insecurity, especially for women, single persons, people of color, and individuals living in the U.S. South, inner cities, and rural areas. Social Security, a lifetime of work, and accumulated wealth are essential to keeping elderly Americans from poverty. For many Americans who will age over the

next two decades, neither earned income nor accumulated wealth are guaranteed in the future to prevent their descent into poverty.

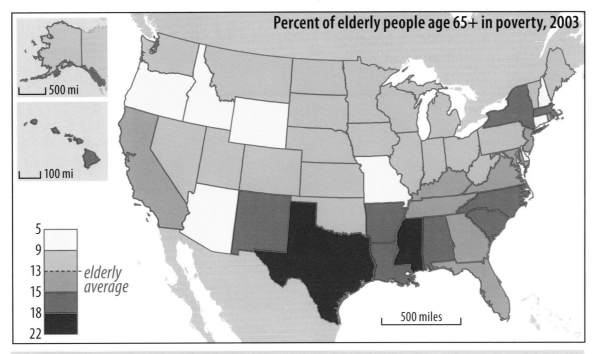

Percent of elderly people age 65+ in poverty, 2003

500 mi

100 mi

5
9
13 — *elderly average*
15
18
22

500 miles

Map 27. *States in the South have high rates of elderly poverty*

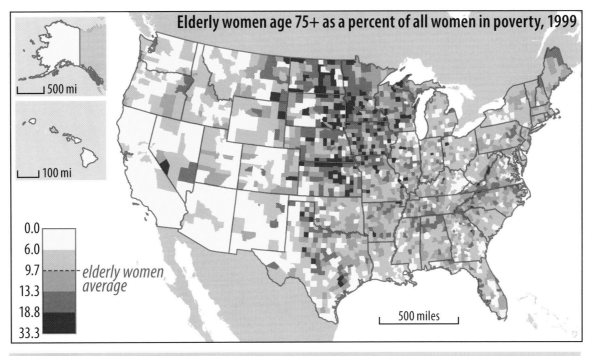

Elderly women age 75+ as a percent of all women in poverty, 1999

500 mi

100 mi

0.0
6.0
9.7 — *elderly women average*
13.3
18.8
33.3

500 miles

Map 28. *Elderly female poverty is high in the Great Plains*

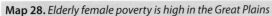

Working But Poor

Over the last two decades, the United States has seen a substantial increase in the number of persons and families who are working but poor. The working poor are individuals who spend at least 27 weeks in the labor force (working or looking for work), but whose incomes fall below the official poverty level (Table 22). These are not individuals who choose voluntarily to work part-time or only part of a year. Instead, these are persons who would work full-time, 40-hour week jobs if that type of employment was available. Of the more than 35 million persons classified as living in poverty in the U.S., most are children, disabled, or elderly, but about seven million of them, men and women, fathers and mothers, young women and men, are working at jobs that do not pay a wage they can live on over the course of a year.

	All people			People below poverty level		
Age	Total	Male	Female	Total	Male	Female
16+	130,143	74,316	63,827	6,802	3,275	3,526
16–19	4818	2,483	2,365	506	232	274
20–24	13,011	6,854	6,157	1,292	545	747
25–34	31,307	17,248	14,059	1,988	953	1,035
35–44	36,368	19,611	16,757	1,581	782	799
45–54	32,120	16,949	15,179	922	501	421
55–64	16,008	8,599	7,409	443	231	212
65+	4,473	2,572	1,669	70	32	38
25–54	99,795	53,808	45,995	4,491	2,236	2,255

Numbers in thousands

Table 22. *The majority of working poor are between ages 25 and 54*

The Demography of the Working Poor

Almost 20% of the working poor are young persons, 10% of those ages 16–19 are working but poor, while 9.9% of individuals ages 20–24 are working and poor. Poor young persons of color are twice as likely to be working and poor as are young white persons (23%, blacks; 14%, Hispanics; compared with 8.8%, whites). And yet the majority of persons who are working and poor are over the age of 24 and are in the prime wage-earning period of life. Women are more likely than men to be working and poor (5.5% vs. 4.4%).

Education, to some degree, is the road out of working and being poor. Only 1.5% of college graduates are working and poor whereas 5.8% of high school graduates and 13.1% of non-high school graduates do not make a living wage (Table 23).

		Rate	
Educational attainment	Total	Male	Female
Total age 16+	4.9	4.4	5.5
Less than HS diploma	13.1	11.6	15.4
Less than 1 year of HS	15.5	15.4	15.9
1–3 years of HS	12.6	10.5	15.7
4 years of HS, no diploma	8.8	6.5	12.6
HS grads, no college	5.8	4.9	7.0
Some college, no degree	4.4	3.6	5.2
Associate degree	2.6	2.0	3.2
College grads	1.5	1.6	1.5

Persons in the labor force for 27 weeks or more: Poverty status by educational attainment and sex, 2001

Table 23. *Education reduces the likelihood of working but being poor*

The Geography of the Working Poor

The working poor in America are found in every state (Map 29). In 17 states, the majority of persons who live in poverty and yet are working totals more than 50%. States where a job fails to pay a living wage are concentrated in the Farm Belt, where economic decline has been ongoing for the last twenty years, and in the West, where population growth has helped keep wages low (Map 30). Working poor families with children are even more concentrated geographically in the South, Southwest, and the western Plains states (Map 31).

In most parts of the country, low levels of income are directly tied to the types of jobs generated in the economy. Today, almost 25% of all jobs are considered low wage. In twelve states, the percentage of all jobs that pay poverty wages is greater than 30%.

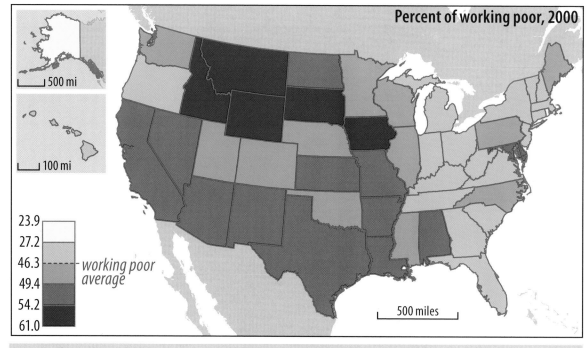

Map 29. *The working poor live in every state in the nation*

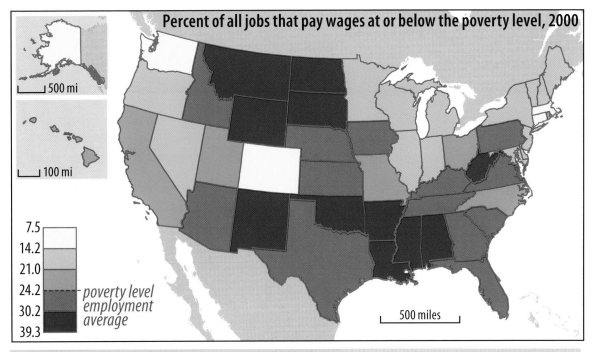

Percent of all jobs that pay wages at or below the poverty level, 2000

500 mi

100 mi

7.5
14.2
21.0
24.2 — poverty level
employment
30.2 average
39.3

500 miles

Map 30. *Percent of all jobs that pay wages at or below the poverty level*

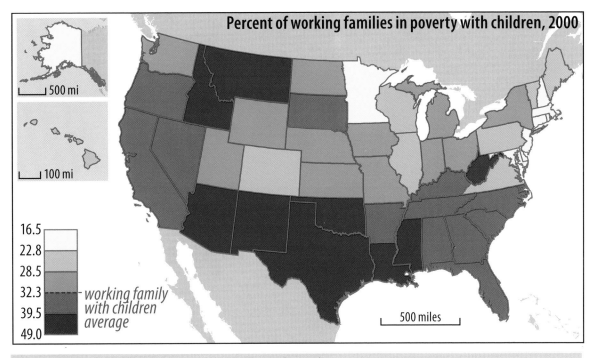

Percent of working families in poverty with children, 2000

500 mi

100 mi

16.5
22.8
28.5
32.3 — working family
with children
39.5 average
49.0

500 miles

Map 31. *Many working poor families with children are in the South*

The Lived Experience of the Wealthy in America

The lived experience of the wealthy in America is in stark contrast with that of the nation's less fortunate. The wealthy live among themselves and have very high incomes compared with the population at large. According to the best data available on tax trends in recent decades, between 1979 and 2000 the average after-tax income of the richest 1% of Americans increased by $576,000, nearly a 200% increase (Figures 42 and 43).

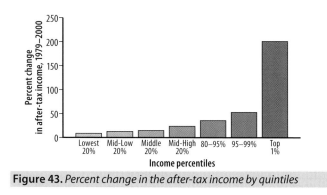

Figure 42. *Gain in income held by top 1%, 1979–2000*

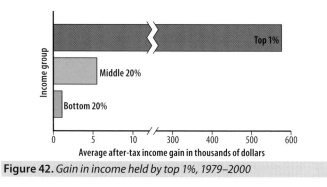

Figure 43. *Percent change in the after-tax income by quintiles*

Geography of Wealth

Income inequality and the distribution of family wealth is a remarkably geographic phenomenon. In rich communities people tend to have a higher and more homogeneous income structure. Further, the very wealthy tend to live near one another to the exclusion of others—our analysis shows that over the 1990–2000 decade, the spatial concentration at both ends of the income spectrum continued.

The geography of wealth in America is concentrated by type of location—metro versus nonmetro—but also is regionally quite distinct. The spatial distribution of rich counties is heavily weighted toward the western and eastern United States, with a significant presence of suburban counties surrounding midwestern cities (Maps 32 and 33).

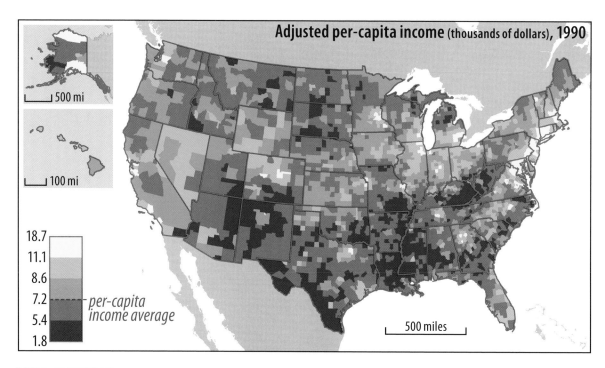

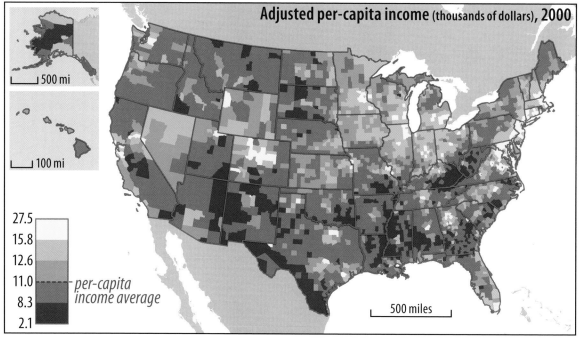

Maps 32 and 33. *Adjusted per-capita income in 1990 and 2000*

To examine wealthy families, using 1990 and 2000 census data we calculated a measure of per-capita adjusted income that equaled median household income minus median housing costs divided by the number of persons per household. Thus our measure reflects per-capita income adjusted for variations in the cost of living, based on average house price including mortgage and maintenance costs, or for renters, the average rent level. We also adjusted for median size families.

The richest of all families live in some of the nation's largest metropolitan regions, including San Francisco, New York, Chicago, and Washington, DC With the exception of cities such as New York and Los Angeles, the vast majority of the wealthy live in suburban enclaves that are proximate to, but outside the inner core of, the nation's largest cities (Table 24).

The nation's capitol tops the list of metro regions with a large number of counties whose residents include those with the highest incomes in the nation. There is surprising stability in the nation's most wealthy communities. Few of the truly rich communities in the 1990s lost place in 2000. Rich communities that have lost favor are associated with old industrial regions and relatively wealthy enclaves in Alaska.

As the nation's income distribution has pulled apart, further separating rich from poor over the 1990s, so too have the nation's poor communities emerged as predominantly southern, Appalachian, and rural. The nation's traditionally poor regions are becoming relatively more so over time.

Rank of affluent counties based on adjusted per-capita income, 2000

Rank: Top thirty				Rank: Bottom thirty			
2000	(1990)		PCI*	2000	(1990)		PCI*
1	(1)	Los Alamos, NM	$27,463	3141	(3114)	Buffalo, SD	$2,126
2	(2)	Falls Church City, VA	25,227	3140	(3141)	Starr, TX	3,157
3	(3)	Fairfax, VA	23,740	3139	(3140)	Shannon, SD	3,670
4	(9)	Hunterdon, NJ	23,520	3138	(3133)	Zavala, TX	3,800
5	(15)	Douglas, CO	23,255	3137	(3112)	Ziebach, SD	3,919
6	(16)	Loudoun, VA	23,145	3136	(3139)	Holmes, MS	4,180
7	(4)	Somerset, NJ	22,510	3135	(3129)	Todd, SD	4,263
8	(7)	Morris, NJ	22,348	3134	(3134)	Maverick, TX	4,286
9	(8)	Arlington, VA	22,025	3133	(3115)	Wilcox, AL	4,361
10	(6)	Howard, MD	21,875	3132	(3109)	Clay, KY	4,377
11	(12)	Marin, CA	21,483	3131	(3138)	Owsley, KY	4,535
12	(26)	Hamilton, IN	21,298	3130	(3073)	Brooks, TX	4,667
13	(34)	Collin, TX	21,262	3129	(3075)	Martin, KY	4,710
14	(5)	Montgomery, MD	21,152	3128	(3019)	Kalawao, HI	4,830
15	(10)	Fairfax City, VA	20,335	3127	(3084)	Sioux, ND	4,933
16	(128)	Delaware, OH	20,228	3126	(3136)	Jefferson, MS	4,958
17	(185)	Forsyth, GA	19,988	3125	(3116)	Knox, KY	4,960
18	(23)	Fayette, GA	19,915	3124	(3093)	Hidalgo, TX	4,963
19	(56)	Pitkin, CO	19,853	3123	(3012)	Wliiacy, TX	5,038
20	(48)	Livingston, MI	19,844	3122	(3066)	Corson, SD	5,067
21	(75)	Williamson, TN	19,839	3121	(3113)	Issaquena, MS	5,085
22	(29)	Oakland, MI	19,814	3120	(3128)	Humphreys, MS	5,117
23	(13)	Alexandria City, VA	19,733	3119	(3132)	Apache, AZ	5,130
24	(59)	Washington, MN	19,687	3118	(3118)	Presidio, TX	5,139
25	(17)	Putnam, NY	19,684	3117	(3089)	McKinley, NM	5,150
26	(20)	DuPage, IL	19,652	3116	(2802)	Bronx, NY	5,175
27	(35)	Chester, PA	19,525	3115	(3076)	McDowell, WV	5,206
28	(30)	Johnson, KS	19,482	3114	(3051)	Hudspeth, TX	5,223
29	(223)	Aleutians West, AK	19,460	3113	(3122)	Magoffin, KY	5,246
30	(62)	Ozaukee, WI	19,300	3112	(3108)	Sumter, AL	5,284

*Per-capita income=(median income - median gross rent) / average household size)

Table 24. *Wealthy are concentrated in suburbs of major metro areas*

HISTORY OF POVERTY

1960s • 1970s • 1980s • 1990s • 2000

Poverty in the 1960s

Who were the poor in the 1960s, and how did they come to be impoverished? A factory closure, illness, lack of transportation, lack of childcare, and other non-behavioral explanations led to poverty. Almost two-thirds of the non-elderly poor worked in the 1960s. Of those who did not work (30%), nearly one-third were ill or disabled. Women, children and those seeking education made up the majority of the rest of the non-working poor. All told, less than 3% of the potential labor pool could have freely chosen not to work.

What It Meant to be Poor in the 1960s

Being poor in 1960 meant getting by on less than $3,553 for a family of four per year, and slightly less for those who lived on a farm ($3,034) (Table 25). The average poor family of four had access to $285 per month in income compared with $653 for a moderate-income family of four. Even given the modest level of income considered sufficient to lift a family of four out of poverty, more than 70% of poor families in the 1960s made incomes $500 under the poverty threshold and nearly 50% made incomes $1,000 below the poverty threshold.

Poverty thresholds, 1968

Family size	Poverty threshold	
	Nonfarm	Farm
1	$1,748	$1,487
2	2,262	1,904
3	2,774	2,352
4	3,553	3,034
5	4,188	3,577
6	4,706	4,021
7+	5,789	4,916

Table 25. *Poverty threshold based on family size and farm residence*

Poverty Level Income Insufficient to Cover the Essentials

Poor families in the 1960s were not expected to own a car or have a bed for each family member, and nothing was budgeted for medical care or insurance. However, according to 1966 data, most of the poor worked (Table 26). A poor family's housing budget provided less than $100 a month for rent,

Work experience of poor non-aged family heads and unrelated individuals, by sex, 1966

(Numbers in millions)	Families		Unrelated individuals	
	Male head	Female head	Male	Female
Total	2.9	1.6	0.7	1.4
Worked	**2.4**	**0.8**	**0.5**	**0.8**
40 weeks+	1.8	0.4	0.2	0.4
Full-time	1.6	0.3	0.2	0.3
Part-time	0.2	0.1	0.1	0.1
<40 weeks	0.6	0.4	0.3	0.4
Full-time	0.5	0.3	0.2	0.2
Part-time	0.2	0.2	0.1	0.2
Did not work	0.5	0.7	0.2	0.6
Ill, disabled	0.3	0.1	0.1	0.2
Couldn't find work	*	*	*	*
Other reasons	0.2	0.6	0.1	0.4
In school	0.1	*	*	*
Housekeeping	*	0.6	*	0.3
All others	0.1	*	*	*

*Less than 50,000   Columns do not add to totals due to rounding

Table 26. *Most of the poor in the 1960s were employed*

utilities, and other housing-related costs such as repairs. No allowance was made for furnishings. No adjustments were made for differences due to climate and the need for heating.

At the time, 25% of poor families were thought to have inadequate diets, lacking access to fresh fruits and vegetables and only limited quantities of protein. The family food budget was drawn notoriously tight with no flexibility for food prepared and consumed outside the home. The average school lunch program allocation per meal was higher than that available to members of poor families. In 1965, 65% of families with incomes under $3,000 had inadequate diets. According to a 1967 federally calculated monthly family budget for an urban family of four, one dollar per day per person was allocated for food (Table 27).

Income inequality hit a high point in 1962, primarily due to the continued losses of jobs in agriculture, which left farm families at risk. It would take another decade before major changes in income distribution saw the lowest fifth of the population

Monthly budgets, poor and moderate income urban families of four, 1967

Consumption item	Poor	Moderate
Total	$285	$653
Food	122	175
Housing	91	199
Transportation	6	77
Clothing & personal care	57	82
Medical care	–	40
Gifts & contributions	–	21
Life insurance	–	13
Other consumption	9	46

Table 27. *Being poor meant going without essentials*

gain relative shares compared with higher-income population groups (Figure 44).

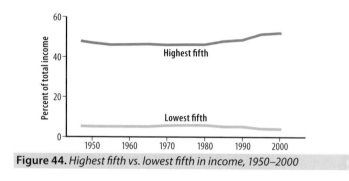

Figure 44. *Highest fifth vs. lowest fifth in income, 1950–2000*

The Demography of Poverty

In the early 1960s, 25 million people or 22% of the population were poor (Figure 45). Over the post-war period, the figure had declined by almost 9%, but a significant number of people in the country were still poor according to employment, household income, and related standards.

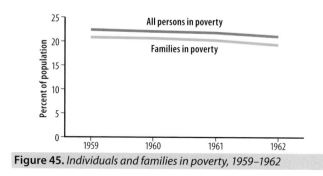

Figure 45. *Individuals and families in poverty, 1959–1962*

In the 1960s, more than one in ten persons lived in severe poverty, with few prospects for a better life. Those who found themselves in poverty were predominantly children, working-age persons, and the elderly. In 1966, 43.5% of the poor were less than 18 years of age, 24.7% were between the ages of 22–54, and another 18% were of retirement age (Table 28).

Selected characteristics of the poor and the non-poor, 1966					
		Numbers (in millions)		Percent distributions	
		Poor	Non-poor	Poor	Non-poor
Age	Total	30.0	163.9	100.0%	100.0%
	<18	13.0	57.4	43.5	35.0
	18–21	1.6	10.4	5.3	6.4
	22–54	7.4	68.7	24.7	41.9
	55–64	2.5	14.7	8.5	9.0
	65+	5.4	12.6	18.0	7.7
Race	Total	30.0	163.9	100.0%	100.0%
	White	20.4	150.2	68.3	91.6
	Nonwhite	9.5	13.7	31.7	8.4
Family status	Total	30.0	163.9	100.0%	100.0%
	Unrelated individuals	5.1	7.6	17.1	4.6
	Family members	24.9	156.3	82.9	95.4
	Head	6.1	42.8	20.3	26.1
	Spouse	4.1	28.5	13.5	23.5
	Other adult	2.1	17.7	7.2	10.8
	Child <18	12.6	57.3	42.0	35.0
Type of residence	Total	30.0	163.9	100.0%	100.0%
	Farm	2.5	8.5	8.2	5.2
	Nonfarm	27.5	155.4	91.8	94.8
	Rural	11.2	46.7	37.3	28.5
	Urban	18.8	117.2	62.7	71.5

Table 28. *Poor and non-poor, by age, race, family status, and type of residence*

The numerical majority of the poor were white—almost 69%—with the remainder people of color. On a percentage basis, however, a black person was almost three times more likely to live in poverty as a white person (Figure 46). That rate remained largely the same throughout the 1960s. Most of the poor were members of families—82%. Most also lived in non-farm residences, predominantly urban in location.

Female-headed households with children also experienced high rates of poverty (Figure 47). During the same time period, for African American families headed by women, the poverty rate was 70%.

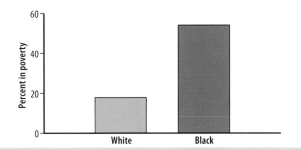

Figure 46. *Percent poverty, white and black persons in the nation, 1959*

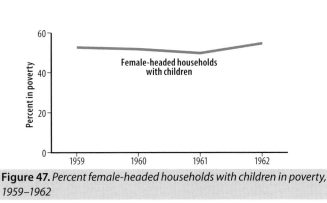

Figure 47. *Percent female-headed households with children in poverty, 1959–1962*

In the mid 1960s, being poor and aged was not uncommon. As many as 6.4 million people over age 65 were poor. Of those, more than one million worked at least part of a year, while more than 500,000 worked full time. The notion of the aged worker was evident even then. Average income in households headed by an aged person was $1,200, slightly less than one third of average family income.

In the 1960s, the working poor were a vital component of the poverty population. Of the 4.5 million non-aged heads of poor families, 1.9 million or 43% worked full time for more than 40 weeks a year. Most of the remaining heads of households also worked at least a portion of the year. Back in 1966, reasons for being working class yet poor were surprisingly well understood: people were poor by chance, the desire to work was strong, but opportunities were not readily available.

America's poor have never failed to work. Since the 1960s, in some classes of jobs and occupations and in certain locations,

work did not pay enough no matter how many hours a person toiled.

The Geography of Poverty

In the 1960s, poverty was geographically concentrated in the South, Appalachia, the U.S.-Mexico border, the Mississippi Delta, and Indian reservations (**Map** 34). Poverty in inner-city urban areas was also high.

Given the high rate of working but poor families, poverty in the early 1960s was only indirectly related to unemployment. High rates of unemployment were found throughout the nation, including the industrial states of the Northeast and the resource-dependent regions of the West (**Map** 35).

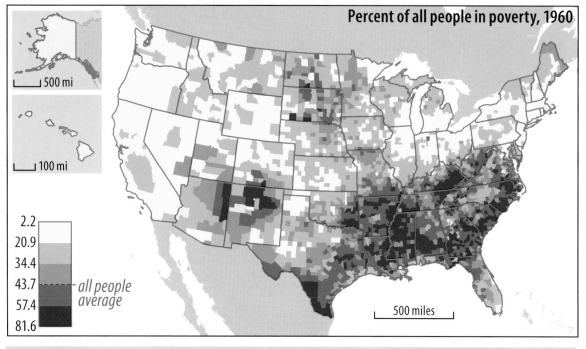

Map 34. *Poverty in America, 1960*

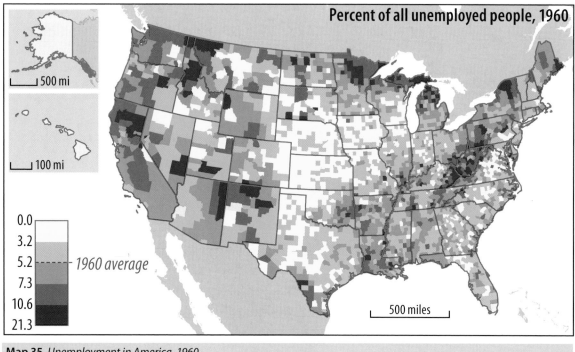

Map 35. *Unemployment in America, 1960*

Poverty in 1970

Programs and policies initiated during the 1960s resulted at the beginning of the 1970s in significant declines in the numbers of persons in poverty and in the numbers of social groups strongly affected by economic uncertainty. Declines were due to an unusual combination of macro-economic trends, poverty policy interventions, and declining income inequality. The greatest change in poverty levels occurred for the elderly.

Child poverty, though declining from a high level in the 1960s, still averaged 20.3% in the 1970s. As portions of the population were lifted out of poverty, children remained vulnerable to economic insecurity, especially in specific regions.

Elderly poverty began to decline in 1966, falling from an average of 28.5% in 1966 to 20.4% in 1970. However, one in five persons over age 64 lived below the federal poverty line.

The geographic location of the poor is correlated with the spatial concentration of different racial groups. Poor whites were concentrated in Appalachia and the Southwest. Black poverty was highly geographically concentrated in the U.S. South. Hispanic poverty was concentrated in the South and U.S. borderlands with Mexico.

The spatial concentration of the persistently poor is even more pronounced under the lens of family poverty. Female-headed households with children living in poverty demonstrate a broader pattern of spatial dispersion, with an evident concentration in the South.

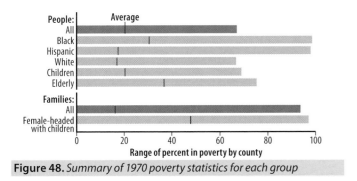

Figure 48. *Summary of 1970 poverty statistics for each group*

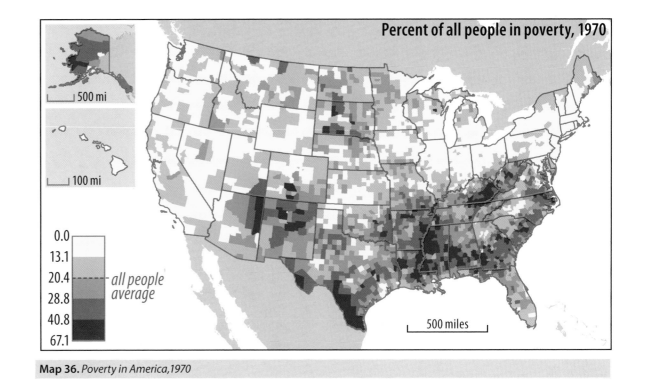

Map 36. *Poverty in America,1970*

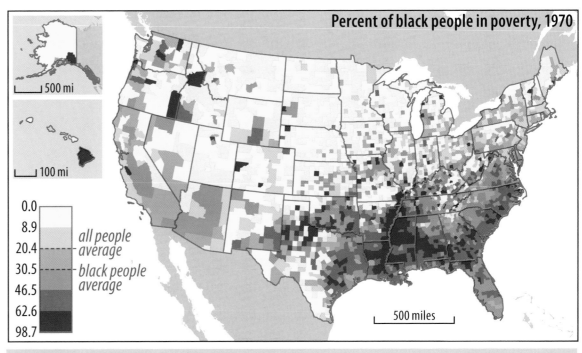

Map 37. *Percent of black people in poverty, 1970*

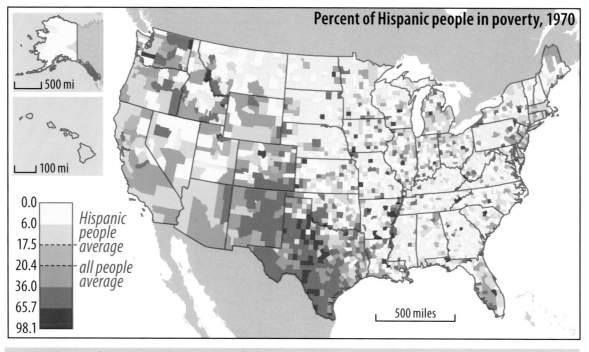

Percent of Hispanic people in poverty, 1970

Legend:
0.0
6.0 — *Hispanic people average*
17.5
20.4 — *all people average*
36.0
65.7
98.1

Map 38. *Percent of Hispanic people in poverty, 1970*

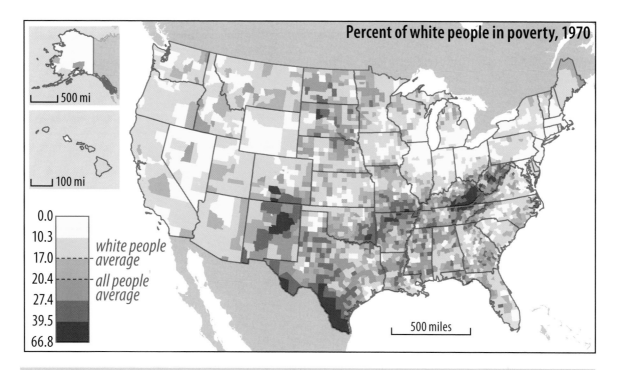

Percent of white people in poverty, 1970

Legend:
0.0
10.3
17.0 — *white people average*
20.4 — *all people average*
27.4
39.5
66.8

Map 39. *Percent of white people in poverty, 1970*

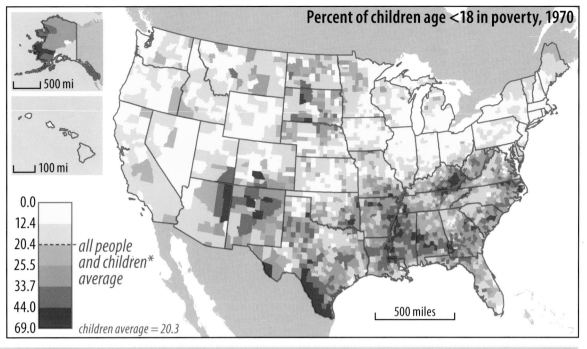

Percent of children age <18 in poverty, 1970

0.0
12.4
20.4 — — all people
25.5   and children*
33.7   average
44.0
69.0   children average = 20.3

500 miles

Map 40. *Percent of children age <18 in poverty, 1970*

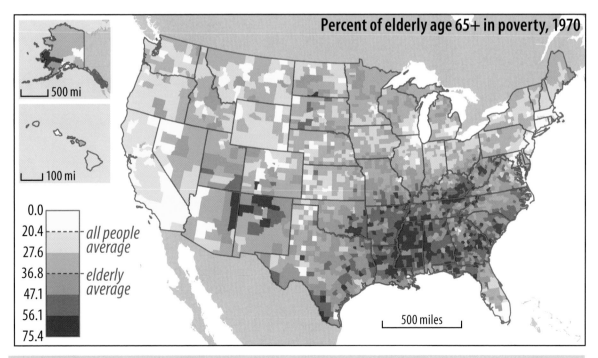

Percent of elderly age 65+ in poverty, 1970

0.0
20.4 — — all people
27.6   average
36.8 — — elderly
47.1   average
56.1
75.4

500 miles

Map 41. *Percent of elderly age 65+ in poverty, 1970*

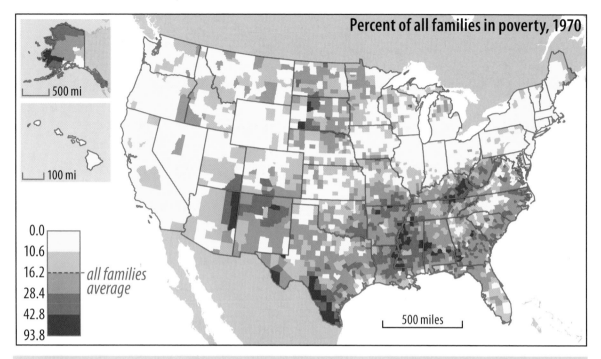

Map 42. *Percent of all families in poverty, 1970*

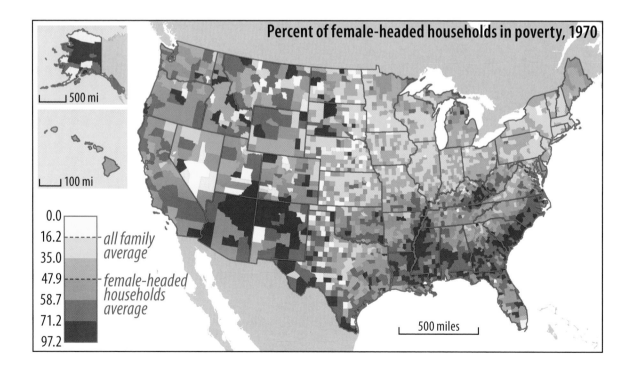

Map 43. *Percent of female-headed households in poverty, 1970*

Poverty in 1980

At the beginning of the 1980s, poverty, which had declined to 11.1% in 1973, had begun to creep upward again. By 1980, the average county poverty rate was 15.8%. Industrial restructuring of the late 1970s brought massive job losses in manufacturing that hit black men very hard. By the early 1980s, one in five black males was unemployed. In the 1980s, inflation and high interest rates resulted in a decline in corporate capital investment in new plant and equipment, which led to high unemployment rates and poverty levels not seen since the 1960s. Elderly poverty rates continued to decline from the previous decade. Rates began to rise for female-headed households with children and young men and women.

Regionally, poverty began to spread across the nation and into the industrial heartland. States in the West experienced increases in their poverty rate over the decade. Black poverty stayed virtually the same, although the spatial distribution of black poverty began to spread out. At the same time, Hispanic poverty began to disperse across the nation and poverty in female-headed households, which had formerly been largely confined to the South and Indian reservations, also began to emerge across the nation. Average white poverty in counties declined over the decade as did family poverty. And yet, many counties throughout the country exhibited poverty rates greatly in excess of the national county average. The economic recession of the late 1970s strongly affected people and families of color, as manufacturing jobs declined in the former industrial heartland of the Northeast and Midwest.

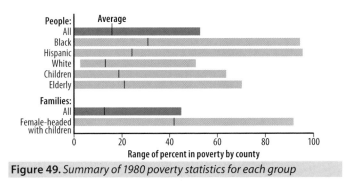

Figure 49. *Summary of 1980 poverty statistics for each group*

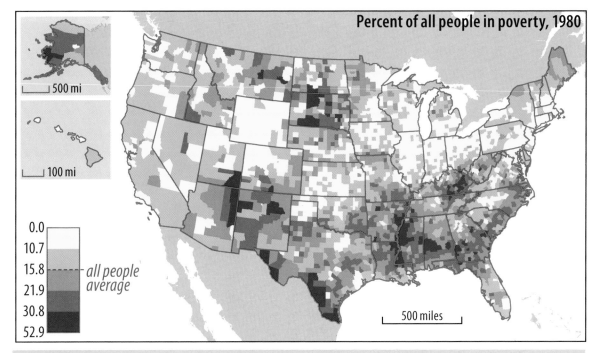

Map 44. *Poverty in America, 1980*

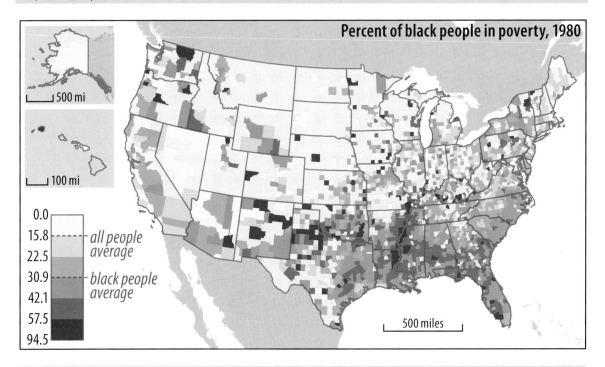

Map 45. *Percent of black people in poverty, 1980*

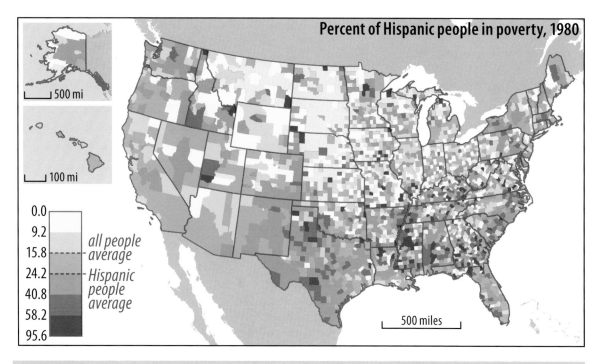

Percent of Hispanic people in poverty, 1980

500 mi

100 mi

0.0
9.2
15.8 — — — *all people average*
24.2 — — — *Hispanic people average*
40.8
58.2
95.6

500 miles

Map 46. *Percent of Hispanic people in poverty, 1980*

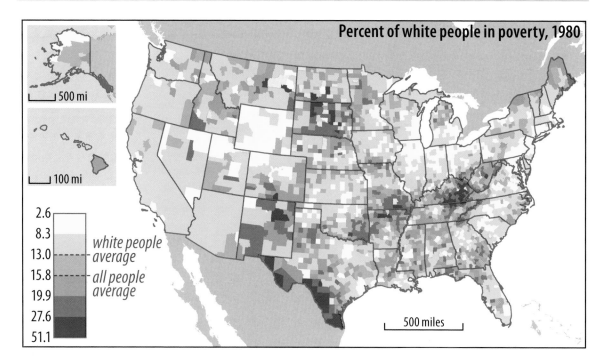

Percent of white people in poverty, 1980

500 mi

100 mi

2.6
8.3
13.0 — — — *white people average*
15.8 — — — *all people average*
19.9
27.6
51.1

500 miles

Map 47. *Percent of white people in poverty, 1980*

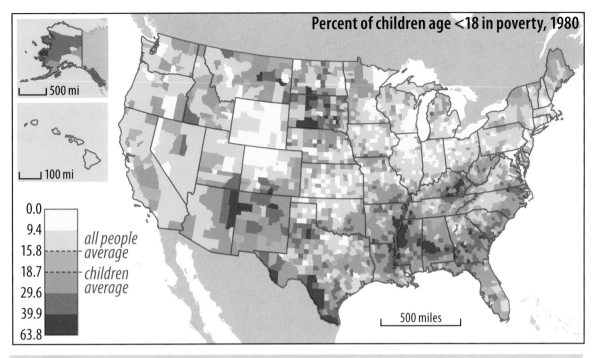

Percent of children age <18 in poverty, 1980

500 mi

100 mi

0.0	
9.4	all people average
15.8	
18.7	children average
29.6	
39.9	
63.8	

500 miles

Map 48. *Percent of children age <18 in poverty, 1980*

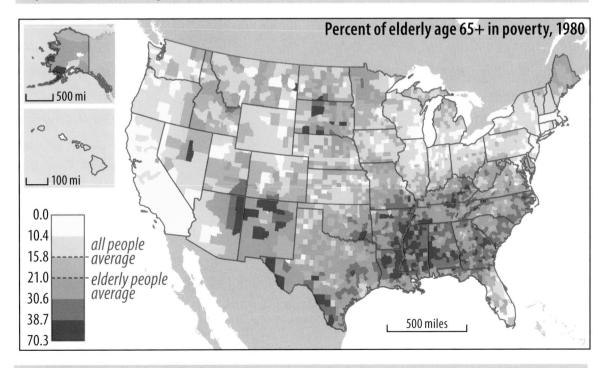

Percent of elderly age 65+ in poverty, 1980

500 mi

100 mi

0.0	
10.4	all people average
15.8	
21.0	elderly people average
30.6	
38.7	
70.3	

500 miles

Map 49. *Percent of elderly age 65+ in poverty, 1980*

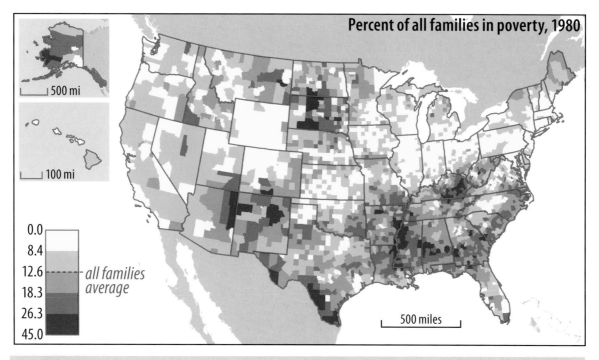

Map 50. *Poverty in America, 1980*

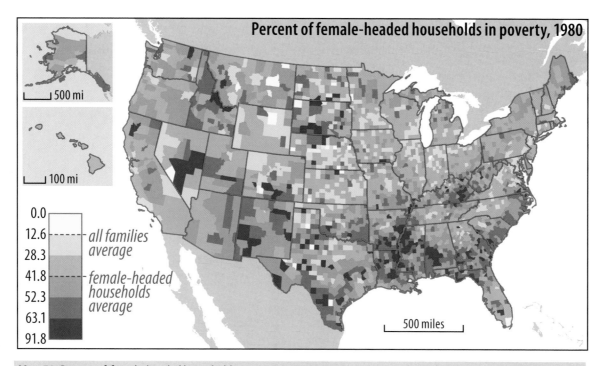

Map 51. *Percent of female-headed households in poverty, 1980*

Poverty in 1990

Poverty remained high throughout the 1980s, with a small decline coming at the end of the decade. By 1990, poverty had begun to rise again, topping 15% by 1993. At no time other than the late 1970s did poverty levels drop below 11%. The number of the nation's poor remained essentially constant since the early 1970s.

Poverty over the 1980s was once again rearranged, with shares more prominent in the South and Southwest. Poverty rates for Blacks and Hispanics were almost double the national average and the geography of their poverty displays distinct concentrations. High county-level poverty for blacks was evident in former manufacturing areas hard hit by industrial restructuring of the previous decade. High county Hispanic poverty was linked to both their historical spatial isolation and the distribution of agricultural regions in the country.

Child poverty grew in the former mining regions of the Southwest and the Great Plains. Concentrations of poor children were found in the central valley of California and in the former timber region of the North. Elderly poverty exhibited a distinct spatial pattern, with the highest concentrations of elderly poor in the southern and south-central regions of the country. Family poverty began to intensify in regions of the U.S. where natural resources were the economic base. Average county female-headed household poverty increased dramatically and uniformly across the country.

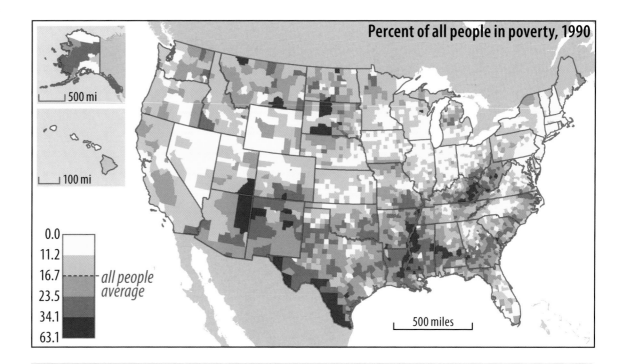

Map 52. *Poverty in America, 1990*

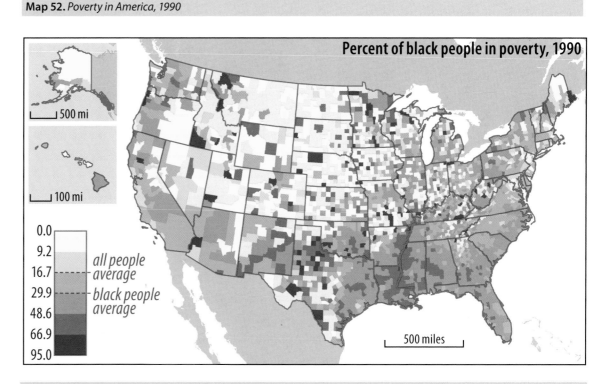

Map 53. *Percent of black people in poverty, 1990*

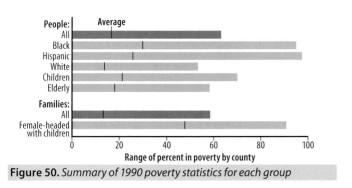

Figure 50. *Summary of 1990 poverty statistics for each group*

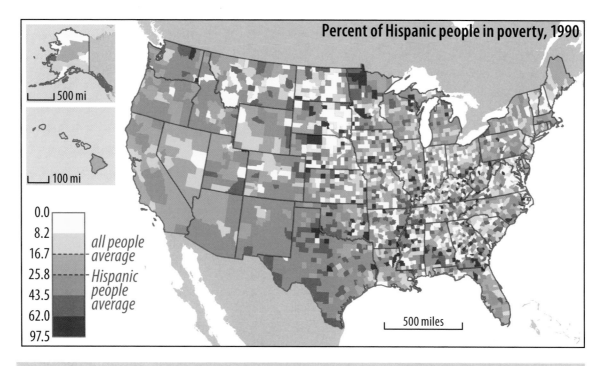

Map 54 *Percent of Hispanic people in poverty, 1990*

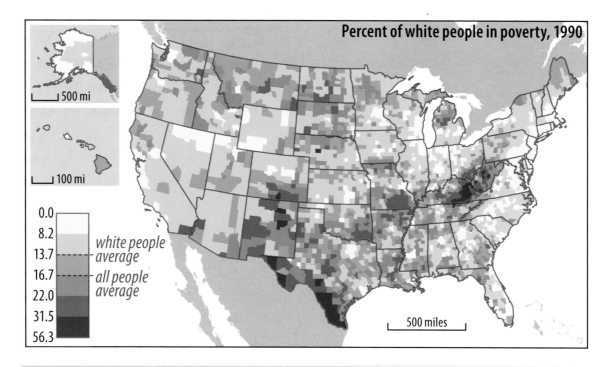

Map 55. *Percent of white people in poverty, 1990*

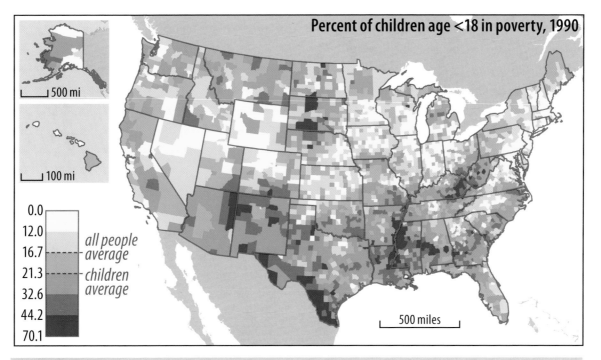

Percent of children age <18 in poverty, 1990

0.0	
12.0	*all people*
16.7	*average*
21.3	*children*
32.6	*average*
44.2	
70.1	

500 mi
100 mi
500 miles

Map 56. *Percent of children age <18 in poverty, 1990*

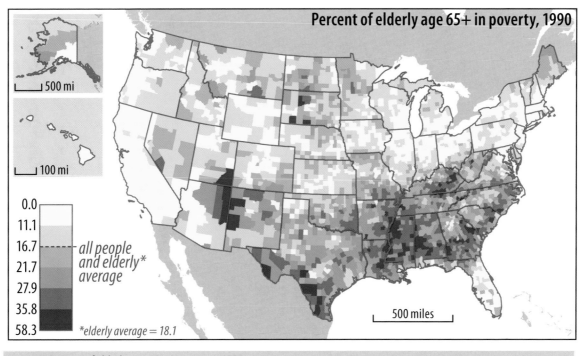

Percent of elderly age 65+ in poverty, 1990

0.0	
11.1	
16.7	*all people*
21.7	*and elderly**
27.9	*average*
35.8	
58.3	

*elderly average = 18.1

500 mi
100 mi
500 miles

Map 57. *Percent of elderly age 65+ in poverty, 1990*

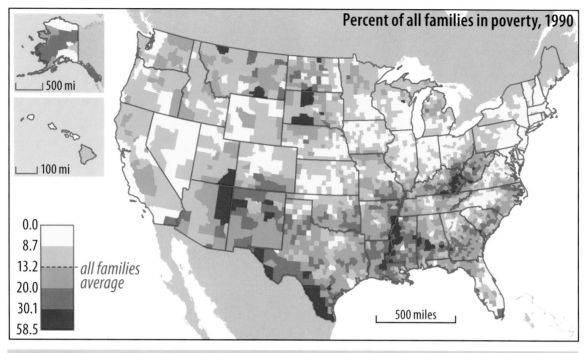

Map 58. *Percent of all famiilies in poverty, 1990*

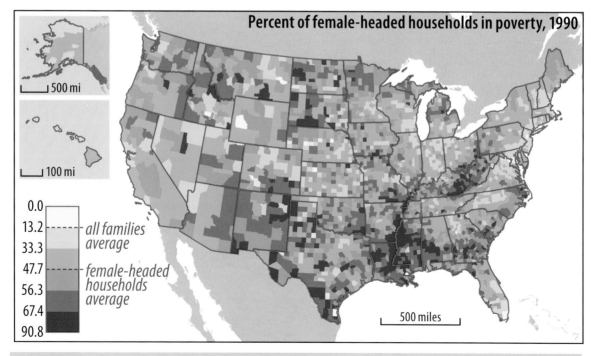

Map 59. *Percent of female-headed households in poverty, 1990*

Poverty in 2000

At the beginning of the 21st century, poverty rates were as high as they were in 1976. A strong economy in the 1990s briefly brought poverty rates down below 12%. In the mid-1990s, two regions—the West and Midwest—saw substantial declines in poverty. At the same time, poverty increased in the South.

By early 2000, poverty rates began to climb again and by 2001 they were back up to levels of the previous decade. Black and Hispanic income levels declined as job losses in manufacturing occurred and new job growth was largely concentrated in low-wage service jobs.

Poverty geography followed the patterns of the 1990s. Black poverty became more dispersed throughout the country. Hispanic poverty began to fill in across the nation. White poverty remained centered in Appalachia, western Texas, and New Mexico. Child poverty continued to be found predominently in the South, Southwest, and parts of the Farm Belt. Elderly poverty, historically quite geographically concentrated in the South, began to disperse and grow, particularly in the traditional Farm Belt. Family poverty increased across the South and Southeast while female-headed household poverty retrenched toward traditional centers of poverty in the South and the Southwest. New pockets of poor female-headed households emerged in Texas and the Farm Belt.

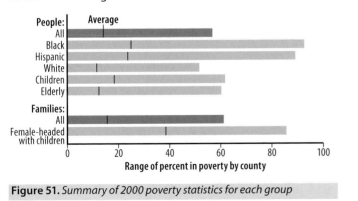

Figure 51. Summary of 2000 poverty statistics for each group

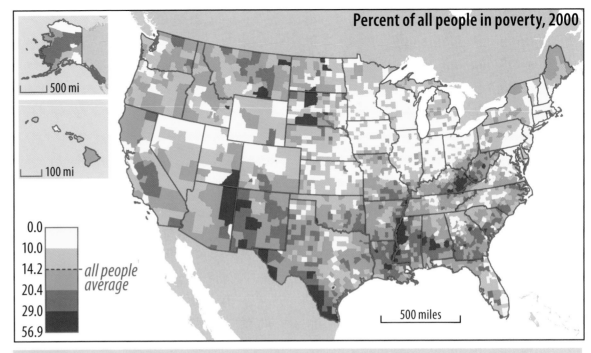

Map 60. Poverty in America, 2000

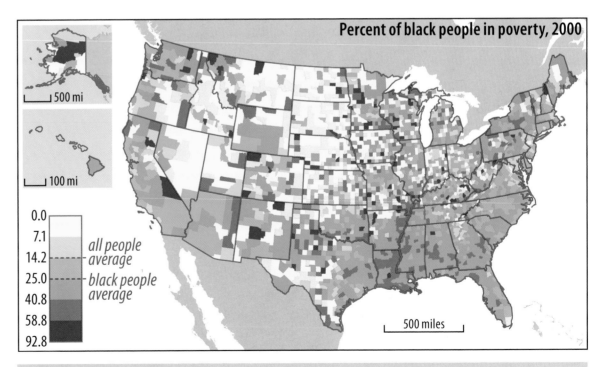

Map 61. Percent of black people in poverty, 2000

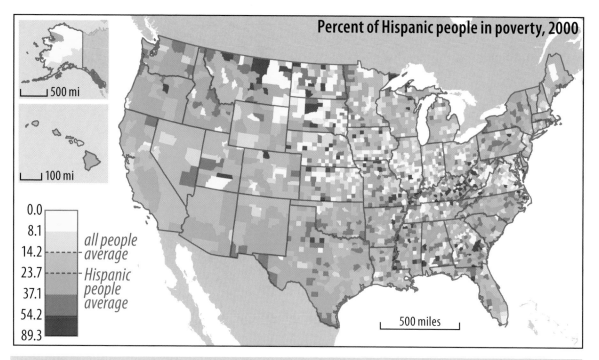

Map 62. *Percent of Hispanic people in poverty, 2000*

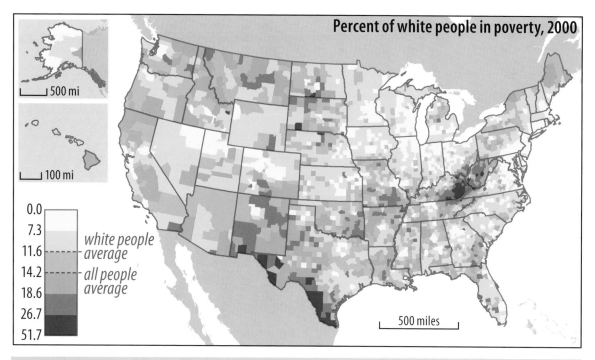

Map 63. *Percent of white people in poverty, 2000*

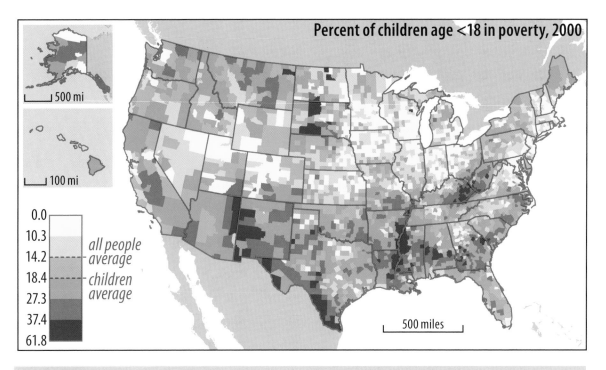

Percent of children age <18 in poverty, 2000

500 mi

100 mi

0.0	
10.3	
14.2	*all people average*
18.4	*children average*
27.3	
37.4	
61.8	

500 miles

Map 64. *Percent of children age <18 in poverty, 2000*

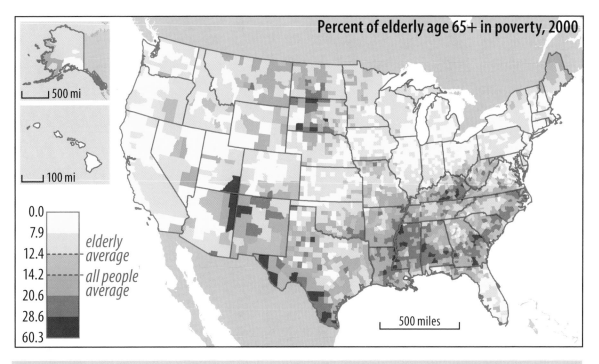

Percent of elderly age 65+ in poverty, 2000

500 mi

100 mi

0.0	
7.9	
12.4	*elderly average*
14.2	*all people average*
20.6	
28.6	
60.3	

500 miles

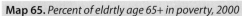

Map 65. *Percent of eldrtly age 65+ in poverty, 2000*

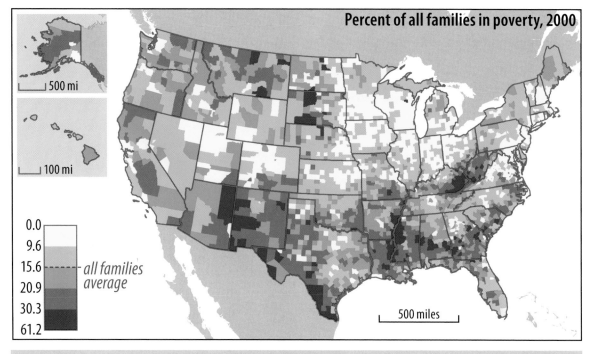

Percent of all families in poverty, 2000

0.0
9.6
15.6 --- all families
20.9   average
30.3
61.2

500 mi

100 mi

500 miles

Map 66. *Percent of families in poverty, 2000*

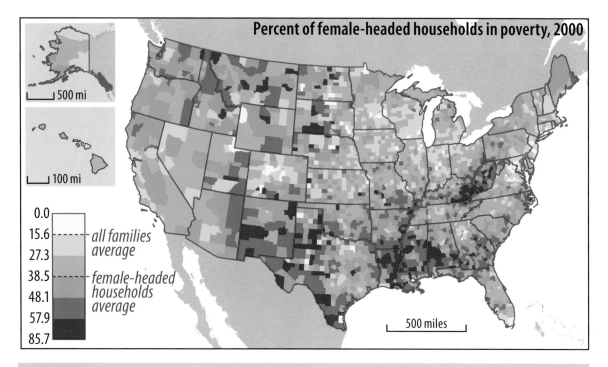

Percent of female-headed households in poverty, 2000

0.0
15.6 --- all families
              average
27.3
38.5 --- female-headed
              households
48.1   average
57.9
85.7

500 mi

100 mi

500 miles

Map 67. *Percent of female-headed households in poverty, 2000*

DISTRESSED REGIONS

Appalachia · Mississippi Delta · Border · Rural · Native American Lands · Segregation

Appalachia: *A Land Apart in a Wealthy Nation*

Appalachia has long been considered one of the poorest regions of the United States. Its rural portions have been persistently mired in poverty for several generations. Many of the region's communities live in isolation, locked out of the prosperity enjoyed by the rest of the nation over the last forty years.

Appalachia's three subregions contain counties in thirteen states from New York in the North to Mississippi in the South. Central Appalachia, the most isolated and poorest part of the region, includes parts of West Virginia, Appalachian Kentucky, the southwestern tip of Virginia, and the northwest part of Tennessee's Appalachian area (Map 68).

Appalachia is home to some of the richest coal mines in the nation (Map 69). Today, one of the most pressing environmental concerns is the mining of coal using a process called "mountain top mining." Coal companies scrape the top off of mountains and pour the over-burden into valley bottoms, damming and destroying streams. People living adjacent to these locations often lose the use of their wells and sometimes their houses collapse due to underground subsidence.

The Appalachian region's manufacturing base has begun to crumble. The state of Georgia lost more than 60,000 manufacturing jobs, most of them in rural parts of the state. Similar patterns affect states across the Appalachian region. Since 1996 the region has lost a total of over 400,000 manufacturing jobs (Figure 52). Much of the job loss occurred in the rural parts of the region.

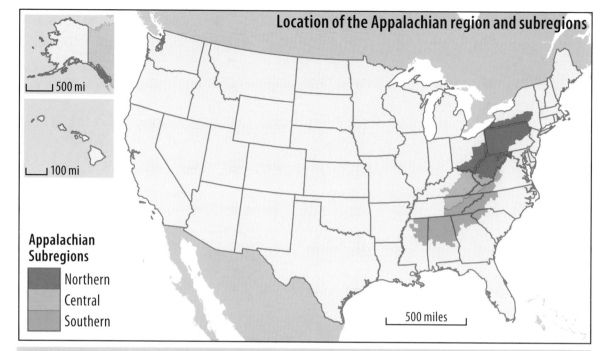

Map 68. *Location of Appalachia and its subregions*

Map 69. *Coal fields in the Appalachian region;* Photo 2. *Mountain top mining in West Virginia*

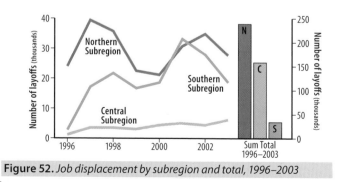

Figure 52. *Job displacement by subregion and total, 1996–2003*

Poverty in the Region

Poverty in Appalachia stems from a complex history of regional economic and political exploitation. The region's poverty rate was once as high as 43% in the 1960s, and still currently exceeds the national poverty rate (Map 70).

Family, Elderly, and Child Poverty

The most vulnerable groups in society are subject to high rates of poverty in Appalachia. The average county family poverty rate is above the national average (18%) (Figure 53). While most elderly in the country live above the poverty line, a significant fraction of the elderly in Appalachia live below the poverty line (Figure 54). In 2000, the average county rate of child poverty in Appalachia was above the national average (Figure 55). In 10% of the region's counties, one out of three children lived in poverty. Rates of child poverty remain stubbornly high in the central part of Appalachia (Map 71).

Poverty and Race

Average county black poverty is higher than white poverty in the Appalachian region (29% vs. 15%). While white poverty

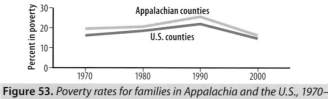

Figure 53. *Poverty rates for families in Appalachia and the U.S., 1970–2000*

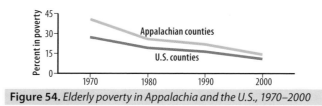

Figure 54. *Elderly poverty in Appalachia and the U.S., 1970–2000*

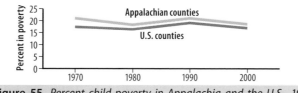

Figure 55. *Percent child poverty in Appalachia and the U.S., 1970–2000*

has declined eight percentage points since 1970, black poverty has changed little over the same period (31% vs. 29%) (Figure 56).

Education

Levels of education in the region have historically been below the national average. The same holds true today (Figure 57).

Education and graduation rates in Central Appalachia remain below the national average in all but a few counties (Map 72). In many counties in the region, high school completion rates for 2000 are still below the national average.

The poorest parts of the region have very low percentages of the population with a college education. In addition, they tend to be located in the North and along the edges of the region (Table 29).

Median Household Income

Median household income in Appalachia is highly skewed spatially, with incomes approaching or exceeding the national average along the edges of the region, while the core sections of Appalachia remain poor. The overall regional income average is below the national average and incomes for blacks are only 60% of the national median (Map 73).

Central Appalachia Lacks Plumbing and Phone Service

Many Appalachian communities lack sanitary water and sewer services. In 2000, over 169,000 housing units had no plumbing. Region-wide, from a high of 14.3% of households lacking complete plumbing in 1970, the figure has dropped to 2.9%. Still, in some counties almost one quarter of the housing units continue to lack complete plumbing (Map 74). While in 1970 almost 50% of the houses lacked phone service, this figure fell to 6% in 2000. And yet, in some parts of the region almost 30% of the houses still do not have phone service.

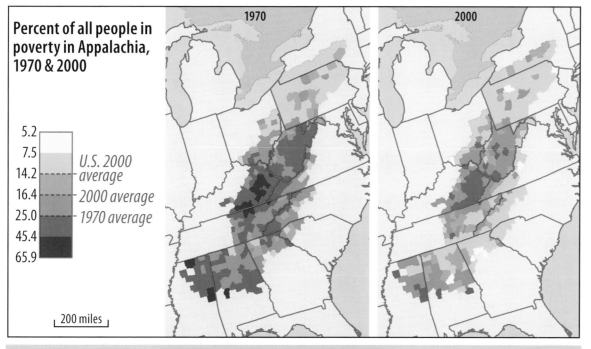

Map 70. *Poverty in Appalachia, 1970 and 2000*

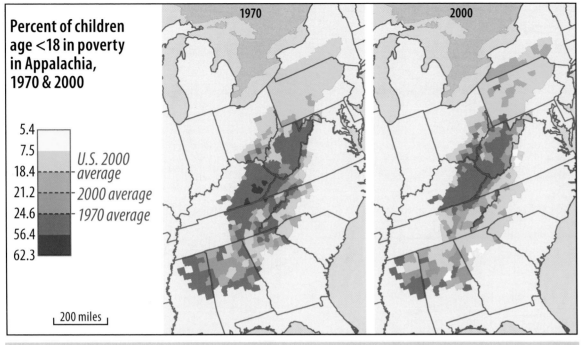

Percent of children age <18 in poverty in Appalachia, 1970 & 2000

5.4	
7.5	*U.S. 2000 average*
18.4	
21.2	*2000 average*
24.6	
56.4	*1970 average*
62.3	

200 miles

Map 71. *Child poverty remains in the central and southern subregions*

Percent of adult population who are college graduates, 1990 and 2000		
	1990	2000
U.S. Total	20.3%	24.4%
Appalachia	14.3	17.7
North	14.4	17.7
Central	8.8	10.7
South	15.4	19.2
Distressed	8.5	10.2
Transitional	13.1	16.1
Competitive	17.4	22.0
Attainment	23.1	29.1

Table 29. *College graduation rates remain below U.S. average*

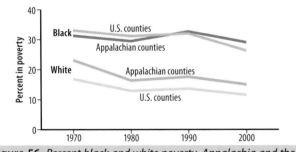

Figure 56. *Percent black and white poverty, Appalachia and the U.S., 1970–2000*

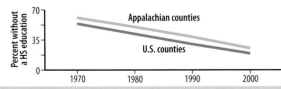

Figure 57. *Percent of the population without a high school education, Appalachia and the U.S., 1970–2000*

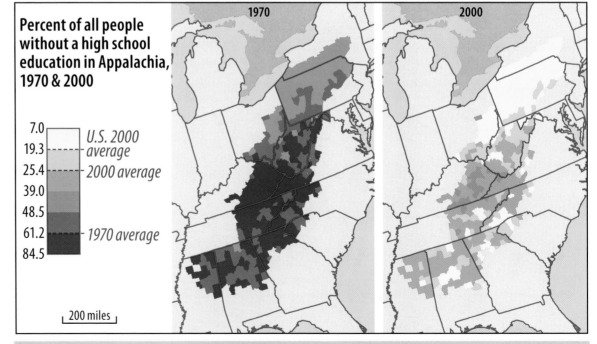

Percent of all people without a high school education in Appalachia, 1970 & 2000

7.0	
19.3	*U.S. 2000 average*
25.4	*2000 average*
39.0	
48.5	
61.2	*1970 average*
84.5	

200 miles

Map 72. *High school completion rates are low*

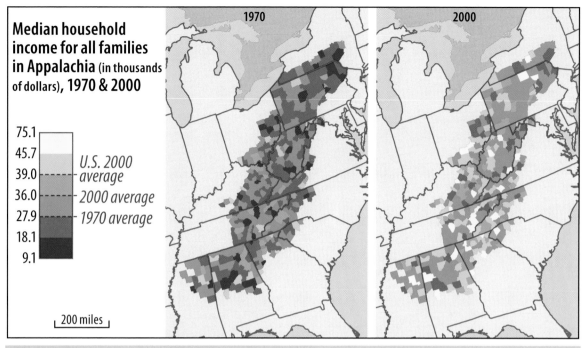

Median household income for all families in Appalachia (in thousands of dollars), **1970 & 2000**

1970   2000

75.1
45.7 — U.S. 2000 average
39.0 — 2000 average
36.0
27.9 — 1970 average
18.1
9.1

200 miles

Map 73. *Median household income in Appalachia, 1970 and 2000*

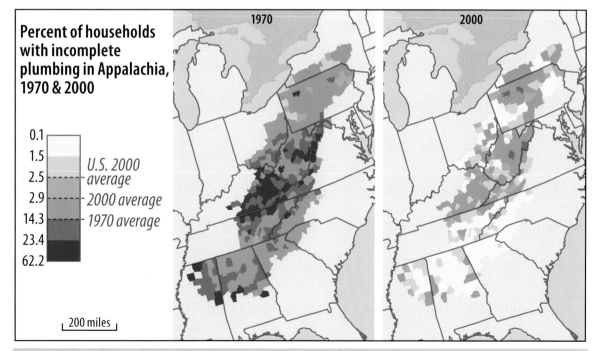

Percent of households with incomplete plumbing in Appalachia, 1970 & 2000

1970   2000

0.1
1.5 — U.S. 2000 average
2.5
2.9 — 2000 average
14.3 — 1970 average
23.4
62.2

200 miles

Map 74. *Percent of households with incomplete plumbing, 1970 and 2000*

The Mississippi Delta: *Plantation Legacy of Slow Growth, Racism, and Severe Inequality*

Persistently slow economic growth, high poverty and illiteracy rates, poor housing and health standards, cultural exclusion, and political and social isolation define the Mississippi Delta region (Map 75).

The system of oppression thought to end with the demise of slavery merely evolved into sharecropping, tenant farming, and Jim Crow laws, ensuring the continued political, economic, and social separation of the region's African American residents. Historically, the region was the site of much of the nation's slavery (Map 76). The Delta remains one of the most segregated regions in the nation.

The Heritage of Cotton

Government intervention to shore up and sustain commodity agriculture prolonged the region's dependence on mono-crop cultivation, and with it a dependence on low-wage agricultural labor (Map 77). This heritage continues to define aspects of the region's economy and society.

Cotton in the Delta Today

Cotton remains a vital crop in the region. Along with aquaculture and soybean cultivation, cotton is still king of the Delta. Along the Mississippi river, in most counties cotton is either the first, second, or third most important crop (Map 78).

Poverty in the Delta

The Delta remains one of the poorest regions in the nation. In 1970, counties along the Mississippi River experienced poverty rates greatly in excess of the national average. These conditions hold to this day (Map 79; Figure 58). The average county poverty rate in the region is still 20.4%.

Black Poverty

Over one-third of the black population lives in poverty (Map 80), with almost one in two rural residents living below the poverty line.

Map 75. *Location of the Delta region*

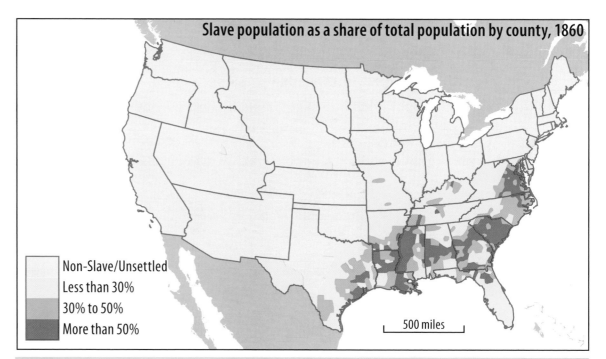

Map 76. *Slave population as a share of total population*

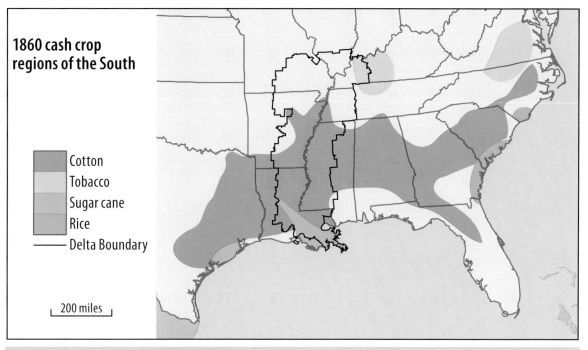

Map 77. *Historical concentrations of agricultural commodities*

1860 cash crop regions of the South

- Cotton
- Tobacco
- Sugar cane
- Rice
- — Delta Boundary

200 miles

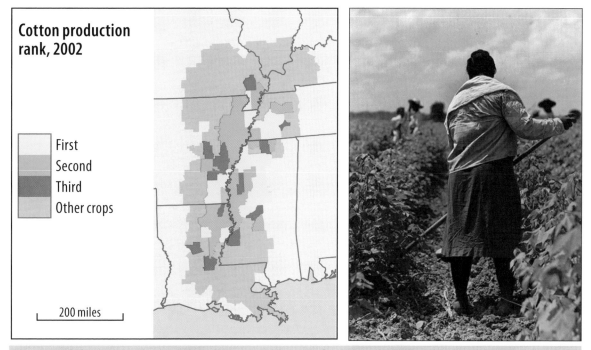

Map 78 and Photo 3. *Cotton continues to be an essential source of income and employment in the Delta, 2002*

Cotton production rank, 2002

- First
- Second
- Third
- Other crops

200 miles

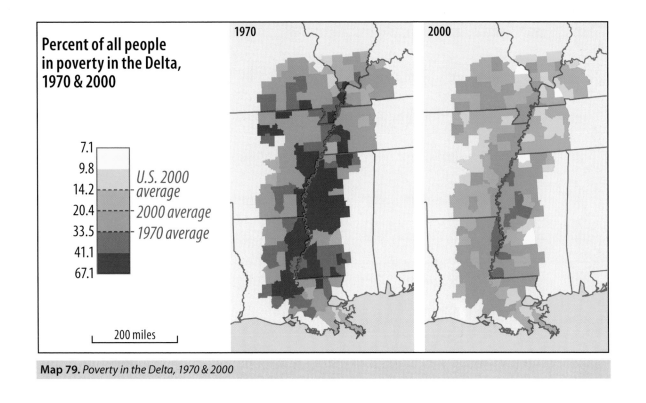

Percent of all people in poverty in the Delta, 1970 & 2000

7.1	
9.8	U.S. 2000 average
14.2	2000 average
20.4	1970 average
33.5	
41.1	
67.1	

200 miles

Map 79. *Poverty in the Delta, 1970 & 2000*

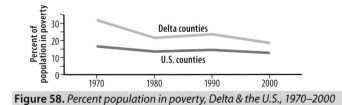

Figure 58. *Percent population in poverty, Delta & the U.S., 1970–2000*

Child Poverty

Child poverty in the Delta is exceptionally high and has been consistently above the national average over the last thirty years. In 1970, 114 out of 218 counties had child poverty rates greater than the mean—31.0% (Map 81). Twenty years later, in 2000, 103 counties had poverty rates greater than the mean of 27.4%. More than 190 counties had child poverty rates above the national average.

Family Poverty

For more than thirty years, family poverty in the Delta has greatly exceeded national averages. Since 1970, Delta family poverty has been 1.5 times the national average (Figure 59).

Family poverty remains highly geographically concentrated along the Mississippi River. The same counties in this region have registered very high rates of family poverty since the 1970s (Map 82).

High School Completion

Long-standing discrimination in education has yielded lower high school completion rates and lower rates of college completion in the Delta population compared with the nation (Map 83). While conditions have improved since the 1970s, the region's high school completion rates still significantly lag behind the national average.

In 2000, 27% of the adult population lacked a high school education (Figure 60). This is almost 30% above the national average. In some counties this figure is as high as 40%—almost double the national average.

Income in the Delta

Black households in the Delta have had consistently lower median incomes compared with white households. In 1970,

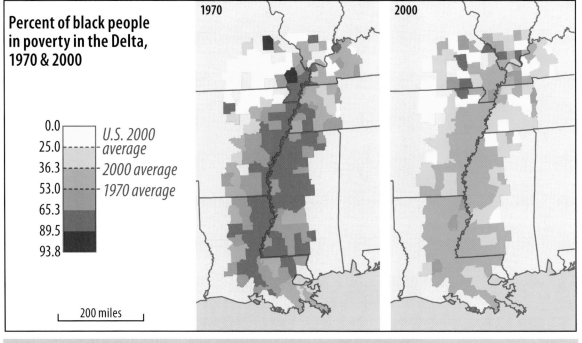

Percent of black people in poverty in the Delta, 1970 & 2000

0.0	U.S. 2000 average
25.0	2000 average
36.3	1970 average
53.0	
65.3	
89.5	
93.8	

200 miles

Map 80. *Percent black living in poverty in the Delta, 1970–2000*

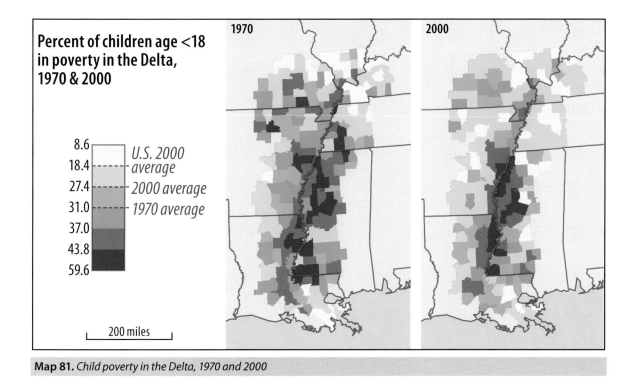

Percent of children age <18 in poverty in the Delta, 1970 & 2000

8.6	U.S. 2000 average
18.4	
27.4	2000 average
31.0	1970 average
37.0	
43.8	
59.6	

200 miles

Map 81. *Child poverty in the Delta, 1970 and 2000*

black median household income was just slightly more than half the white median household income. Despite dramatic increases in median household incomes since the 1970s, only modest progress has been made in reducing the difference between black and white household income levels in the region. In 2000, black household income was two-thirds that of white households in the region (Maps 84 and 85). In some counties the median household income of blacks was 20% of the average white household income for the region.

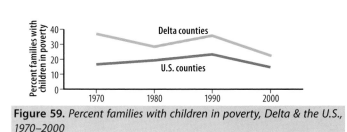

Figure 59. *Percent families with children in poverty, Delta & the U.S., 1970–2000*

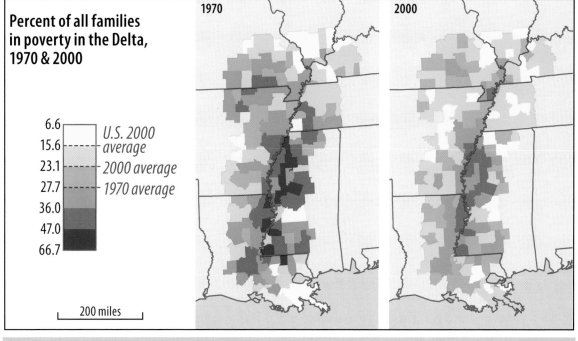

Percent of all families in poverty in the Delta, 1970 & 2000

6.6	U.S. 2000 average
15.6	
23.1	2000 average
27.7	1970 average
36.0	
47.0	
66.7	

200 miles

Map 82. *Family poverty in the Delta, 1970 and 2000*

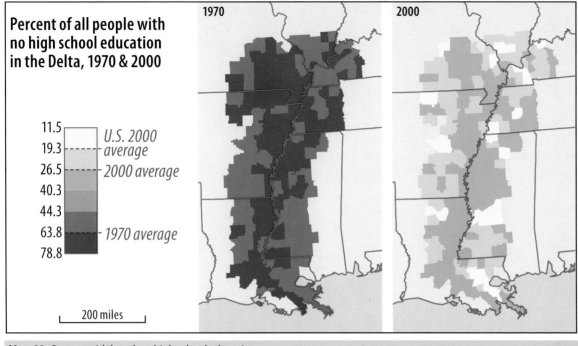

Percent of all people with no high school education in the Delta, 1970 & 2000

1970

2000

11.5	
19.3	*U.S. 2000 average*
26.5	*2000 average*
40.3	
44.3	
63.8	*1970 average*
78.8	

200 miles

Map 83. *Percent with less than high school education*

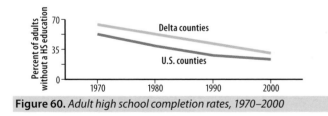

Figure 60. *Adult high school completion rates, 1970–2000*

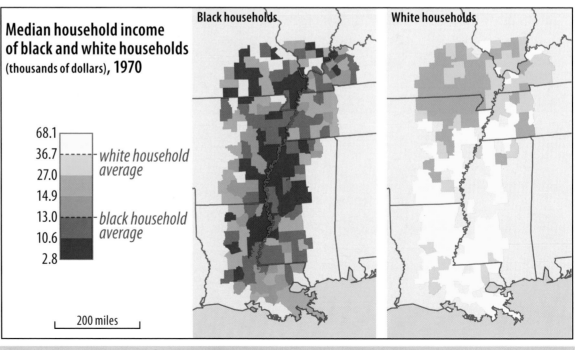

Median household income of black and white households (thousands of dollars), **1970**

Black households

White households

68.1	
36.7	*white household average*
27.0	
14.9	
13.0	*black household average*
10.6	
2.8	

200 miles

Map 84. *Median income for black and white households, 1970*

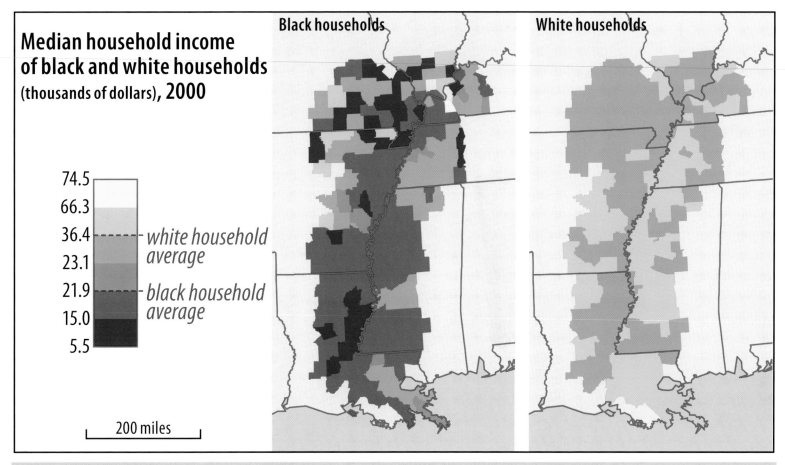

Median household income of black and white households (thousands of dollars), **2000**

Black households

White households

74.5
66.3
36.4 ---- *white household average*
23.1
21.9 ---- *black household average*
15.0
5.5

200 miles

Map 85. *Median income for black and white households, 2000*

First Nation Poverty: *Lost Lands, Lost Prosperity*

There are more than 500 Native American tribes across the nation, numbering more than four million people. Approximately 25% of this population lives on tribal lands or areas designated as Native American lands. These areas are predominantly found in the western U.S., with smaller settlements throughout the nation (Map 86).

More than 29% of those living on tribal lands or reservations live in poverty. Native American poverty is intimately tied to the lack of economic development in those areas.

Per-capita incomes in locations with high concentrations of Native Americans are approximately 20% below the national average (Table 30).

Per-capita income of individuals living on native lands, 1999	Number of people	Per-capita income (1999 dollars)
All counties	3077	$22,138
Metro counties	816	26,358
Nonmetro counties	2261	20,616
Non-Tribal counties	2743	22,282
Tribal counties	367	21,068
Reservation & trust area	263	21,465
OTSA-TDSA area	104	20,071
Tribal counties w/5% or more AI	156	18,649
Reservation & trust area	103	18,902
OTSA-TDSA area	53	18,156

Table 30. *Income levels on tribal lands are below national averages*

Native American Poverty is Evident Throughout the Nation

Poverty rates among Native Americans exceed the national average by more than 9 percentage points. Regardless of where they live, Native Americans experience high rates of poverty relative to the national average (Map 87). Although the concentration of poverty among Native Americans is most evident on tribal lands, poverty rates are high overall, and greatest in the West.

Native American Children are at High Risk of Living in Poverty

The level of poverty among Native American children is significantly higher than the national average. Native American

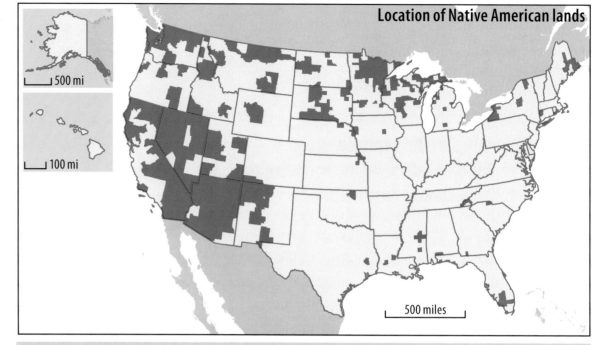

Map 86. *Native American lands*

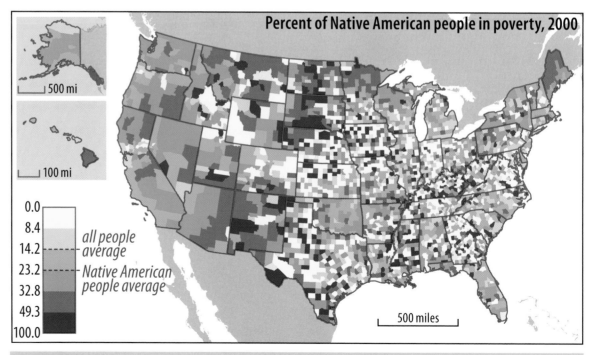

Map 87. *Native American poverty dispersed throughout the nation*

child poverty is more than 40% higher than that for the general population. In some parts of the country, child poverty is five times the national average (Map 88).

Elderly poverty is above the national average in Native American lands counties. In some counties elderly poverty tops 50% of the population over the age of 65 (Map 89).

Native American household poverty is above the national average (Map 90). This relationship has been consistent through time.

The percent of Native American female-headed households with children as a percent of all households in poverty is high relative to the nation. Almost 50% of female-headed households with children live in poverty (Map 91).

Native Americans at Risk: Poor Health and Susceptibility to Disease End Life Early

The health status of Native Americans is significantly lower than that of the rest of the U.S. population. Age-adjusted mortality statistics indicate that Native Americans die at a much higher rate than the non-native population. Thirty percent of the Native American population are under 45 at the age of death (Figure 61).

Native Americans are also unusually susceptible to diabetes. The diabetes mellitus mortality rate for the Indian service area population was almost 40 (per 100,000 population) in 1996, compared with the rate of 11.2 for the entire U.S. population in 1995.

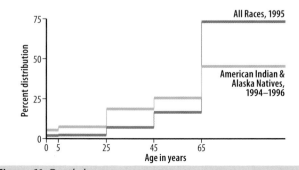

Figure 61. *Death, by age*

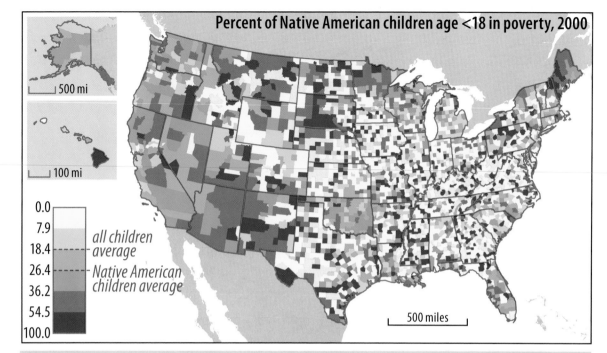

Map 88. *Child poverty has increased over time*

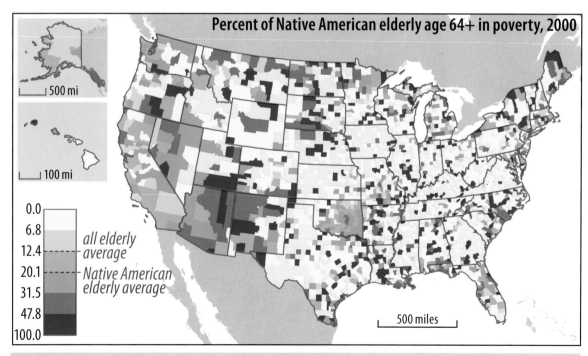

Map 89. *Elderly poverty in counties throughout the nation*

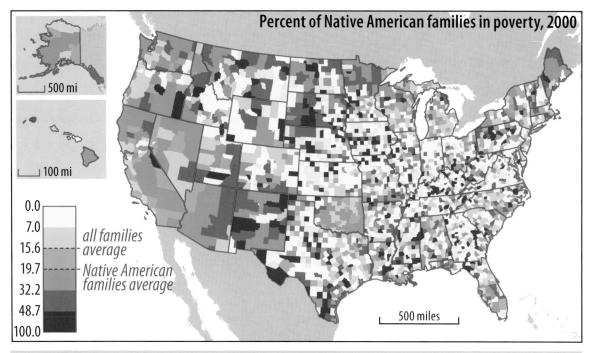

Map 90. *Native American family poverty concentrated in the West*

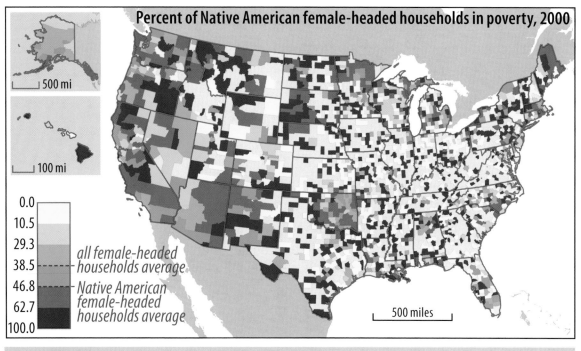

Map 91. *Female-headed households with children in poverty*

Housing Conditions are a Tragedy

Forty percent of Native Americans live in overcrowded or physically inadequate housing conditions, whereas the rate for the general population is 6%. Current estimates indicate an immediate need for 200,000 housing units (Figure 62). Infrastructure needs are overwhelming. One in five homes on reservations lacks complete in-house plumbing, a rate 20 times the national average.

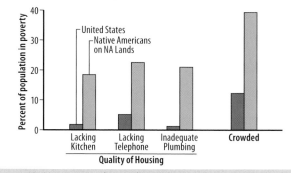

Figure 62. *Housing quality and crowding on Native American lands*

Economic Circumstances of Native Americans

Workers in Native American areas are disproportionately dependent on government employment, and more dependent on Social Security, Supplemental Security, and public assistance than the rest of the country. Of the 2,016,734 households reported in American Indian, Alaska Native, and Hawaiian Homeland (AIANHH) areas in Census 2000, 27% received Social Security; 5.6%, Supplemental Security; and 5.4%, public assistance. Additionally, the proportion of households with income from earnings was slightly less on Native American lands—78.1% as compared to 80.5% of total U.S. households.

Education Continues to Lag

Poor schools and geographic and social isolation contribute to low levels of education and high drop-out rates in the Native American population (Map 92). Approximately 30% of Native Americans 25 years and older do not have high school diplomas compared with less than 20% for the nation as a whole (Table 31). Higher education levels are low, too. The percentage of Native Americans with bachelor's degrees or higher is half the national average.

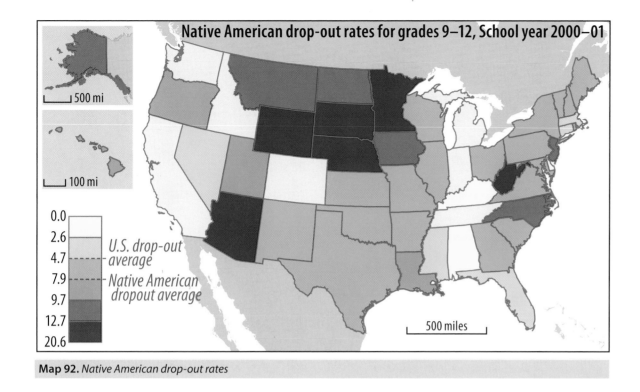

Native American drop-out rates for grades 9–12, School year 2000–01

500 mi

100 mi

0.0
2.6
4.7 ---- *U.S. drop-out average*
7.9 ---- *Native American dropout average*
9.7
12.7
20.6

500 miles

Map 92. *Native American drop-out rates*

The Impact of Gaming

Gaming on Native American lands has received much press in recent years, but the success and ensuing positive economic impact has been felt in only a very small number of areas. In the late 1990s, only 13% of the Class III Indian Casinos studied by the U.S. General Accounting Office accounted for 59% of the revenues gained from tribal gambling. The majority of tribes are not getting wealthy from the gaming industry. Only a few have been successful, and most areas have not attempted involvement in the industry. Not denying the impact of new jobs, jobs in gambling on reservations tend to pay lower wages than non-gambling-related jobs in the same area (Table 32).

Educational attainment (highest level): Percent of population age 25+, 2000			
	Total	Male	Female
Native Americans			
High school graduate or higher	70.9	70.0	71.7
Bachelor's degree or higher	11.5	11.4	11.6
U.S. total			
High school graduate or higher	80.4	80.1	80.7
Bachelor's degree or higher	24.4	26.1	22.0

Numbers in percent

Table 31. *High school and college graduation rates are low for Native Americans*

Average casino salaries vs. surrounding area average wage and salary income, 1996 and 1997			
Tribe	Average wage & salary income for gaming counties 1996	State average wage & salary income for nonmetro areas 1996	Average tribal gaming payroll 1997
Ho-Chunk	$23,375	$21,483	$18,459
Mohegan	$31,242	$27,846	$25,026
Oneida	$26,380	$21,483	$27,761
Sault Ste. Marie Chippewa	$19,924	$22,249	$15,292
Standing Rock Sioux	$17,868	$19,044	$17,107

Table 32. *Casino jobs often pay below local averages*

The Border Region: *Where the Global and the Local Meet*

The borderlands between the United States and Mexico are the home of more than 10 million people, many of whom are immigrants seeking jobs in Maquiladoras and in seasonal industries such as agriculture (Map 93). Border populations are frequently of Hispanic heritage; the majority are American citizens either by birth or length of residency in this country.

Poverty in the Region

Border counties are some of the poorest communities in the U.S. and have been in that condition since the 1970s. The majority of truly poor Border counties in 1970 were in Texas. Conditions have only marginally improved in the interim thirty years (Map 94).

The percent of the population living in poverty in Border counties has been significantly above that for the nation for more than three decades (Figure 63). More than 25% of the population lives in poverty. In the more remote areas of the borderlands, the figures are much higher.

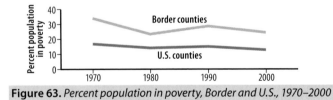

Figure 63. *Percent population in poverty, Border and U.S., 1970–2000*

Child Poverty Along the Border

Child poverty in counties along the Border is almost twice the national average and has changed little since the 1970s (Map 95; Figure 64).

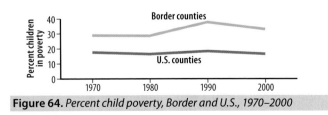

Figure 64. *Percent child poverty, Border and U.S., 1970–2000*

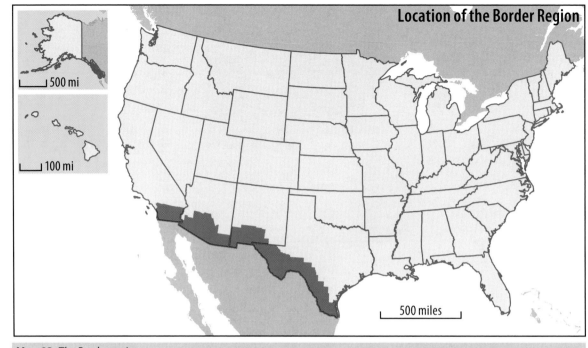

Map 93. *The Border region*

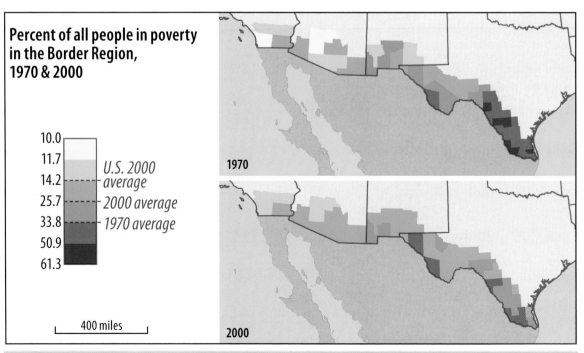

Map 94. *Poverty along the Border, 1970–2000*

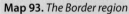

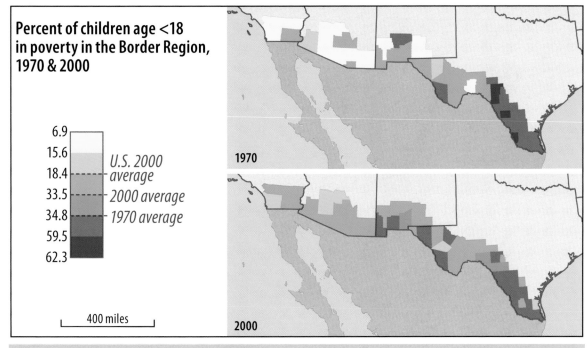

Percent of children age <18 in poverty in the Border Region, 1970 & 2000

6.9
15.6 — *U.S. 2000 average*
18.4 ---- *2000 average*
33.5 ---- *2000 average*
34.8 ---- *1970 average*
59.5
62.3

400 miles

1970

2000

Map 95. *Child poverty along the Border, 1970 and 2000*

Elderly

Elderly persons living in the Border region are twice as likely to live in poverty as elderly persons nationally. In some counties elderly poverty rates exceed 40%.

Family Poverty

Family poverty rates along the Border continue to be almost twice the national average (Figure 65).

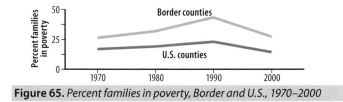

Figure 65. *Percent families in poverty, Border and U.S., 1970–2000*

Female-headed Households Compared with All Families

Hispanic families have traditionally had high rates of two-parent households. More recently, this historic trend has begun to change and there is a growing number of female-headed households with children (Figure 66). Female-headed households with children in poverty, as a share of all female-headed households, are significantly above the national average (Map 96).

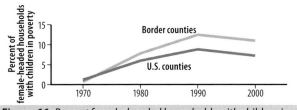

Figure 66. *Percent female-headed households with children in poverty as a share of all households, Border and U.S., 1970–2000*

Hispanic Poverty

Hispanics in the region are more likely to live in poverty compared with Hispanics residing in other areas of the nation (Figure 67).

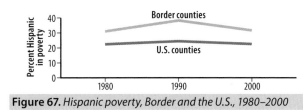

Figure 67. *Hispanic poverty, Border and the U.S., 1980–2000*

High School Completion

The remote location, lack of adequate public services, and transient nature of the population due to the limited employment opportunities nearby, all contribute to the low levels of education in the borderlands population (Map 97; Figure 68).

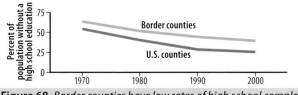

Figure 68. *Border counties have low rates of high school completion*

Unemployment

In the Border region, unemployment rates remain significantly higher than those for the rest of the nation (Figure 69). Over time, rates of unemployment along the Border are increasing relative to the nation.

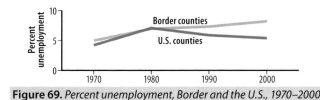

Figure 69. *Percent unemployment, Border and the U.S., 1970–2000*

Income in the Region

Border counties have some of the lowest household incomes in the country. At an average of a little over $25,000 for the entire border area, income is two-thirds the national Hispanic mean (Figure 70; Map 98). Average incomes in Colonia communities, areas where people live in shanties that are often without water or waste disposal, are estimated to be much lower—as little as $5,000 per year.

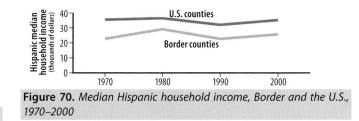

Figure 70. *Median Hispanic household income, Border and the U.S., 1970–2000*

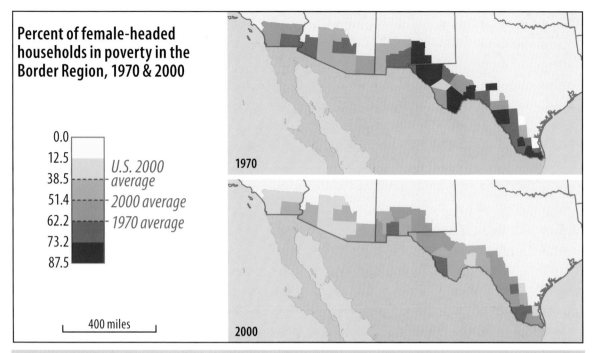

Percent of female-headed households in poverty in the Border Region, 1970 & 2000

0.0	
12.5	*U.S. 2000 average*
38.5	*2000 average*
51.4	*1970 average*
62.2	
73.2	
87.5	

1970

2000

400 miles

Map 96. *Percent female-headed households with children in poverty as a share of female-headed households, Border Region 1970–2000*

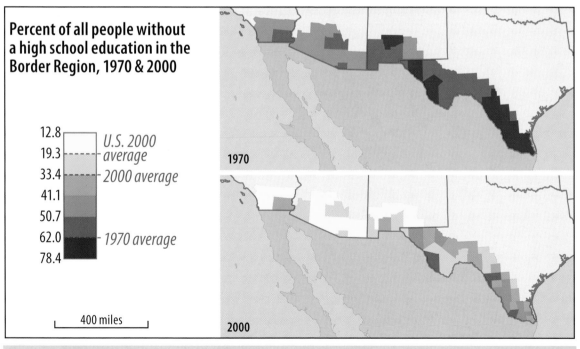

Percent of all people without a high school education in the Border Region, 1970 & 2000

12.8	*U.S. 2000 average*
19.3	*2000 average*
33.4	
41.1	
50.7	
62.0	*1970 average*
78.4	

1970

2000

400 miles

Map 97. *Lack of high school education, Border Region, 1970 and 2000*

Housing Conditions Below National Standards

Housing conditions are often poor along the Border. More than 30,000 Border households lack complete plumbing facilities. Incomplete plumbing facilities in this area are double the national average (Figure 71; Map 99).

Figure 71. *Percent houses without plumbing, Border and the U.S., 1970–2000*

Mobile homes have become an increasing share of residential housing stock. While affordable, such housing loses value rapidly and often becomes a burden to families with low incomes (Figure 72).

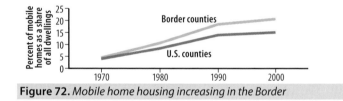

Figure 72. *Mobile home housing increasing in the Border*

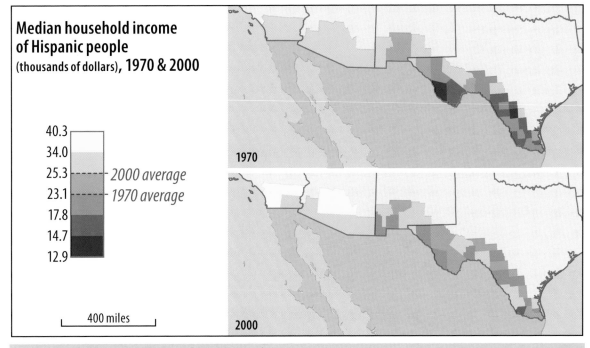

Median household income of Hispanic people
(thousands of dollars), **1970 & 2000**

40.3
34.0
25.3 ---- *2000 average*
23.1 ---- *1970 average*
17.8
14.7
12.9

1970

2000

400 miles

Map 98. *Median household income of Hispanic people*

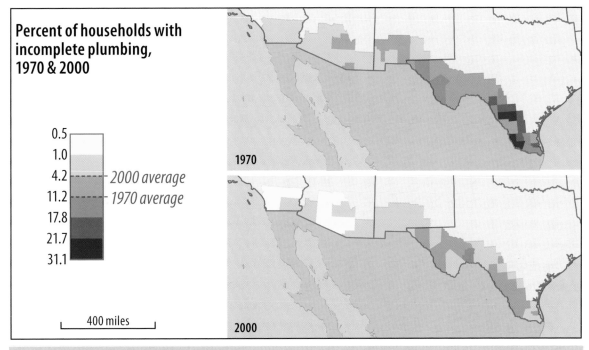

Percent of households with incomplete plumbing, 1970 & 2000

0.5
1.0
4.2 ---- *2000 average*
11.2 ---- *1970 average*
17.8
21.7
31.1

1970

2000

400 miles

Map 99. *Percent of households with incomplete plumbing, Border Region, 1970 and 2000*

Rural Poverty in America

In 1970, almost one in five families in rural America was experiencing poverty. Poverty rates for children and the elderly in rural communities were substantially higher than the national average. In many parts of the country, rural poverty was associated with a declining economic base, as the nation's economy began its final shift away from agriculture and toward manufacturing and services—employment often found in urban areas.

In the last ten years of the 20th century a significant number of rural counties continued to lose population. The decades-old pattern of rural poverty remained intact, even as formerly rural counties on the urban fringe came to be identified as metropolitan. For children, the elderly, people of color, and women-headed households with children, residency in rural areas carried the distinct possibility of living in poverty.

To examine the changing geography and demography of poverty in rural counties of the U.S., we use the Urban Rural Continuum, a county-level coding scheme developed by the U.S. Department of Agriculture's Economic Research Service. The nine-part coding system provides a consistent definition of "rural" based on county population size (degree of urbanization) and adjacency, which facilitates analysis of trends across counties over time. Analysis of 1970 Census data uses the 1974 definition of the Continuum. The 2000 analysis uses the 2003 county definition based on the Continuum.

The Geography of Rural Poverty in 1970

In 1970, poverty was a pervasive experience in rural America. Poverty concentrations were evident in the Piedmont region of the Carolinas, the Mississippi Delta, Appalachia, Indian Reservations, the Border region, and parts of the Plains states. Along the eastern seaboard, the Upper Peninsula of Michigan and the Northern Sierra region of California also exhibited high rates of poverty.

In the 1970s, the rural counties surrounding many of America's southern cities were experiencing high poverty rates and would continue to do so for several more decades (Map 100).

The Demography of Poverty in Rural Communities in 1970

The populations in rural America who were poor in the 1970s included children, the elderly, people of color, and female-headed households (Figure 73). High rates of child poverty in rural areas mirrored those for the overall population. Poor children were most often located in the South and in Appalachia and to a lesser extent Texas. Rates were lower in the Plains states and the California Sierras (Map 101).

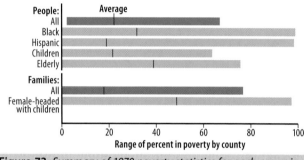

Figure 73. *Summary of 1970 poverty statistics for each group in rural counties*

The Elderly

In 1970, the median level of poverty for the elderly population was almost 30%—substantially higher than that for children. The elderly poor were strongly concentrated in the South, across the south-central states, and scattered in the eastern Plains states (Map 102).

African Americans

In 1970, the majority of African Americans lived in the South. Despite the mass migration of blacks out of the South in the mid 20th century, when more than 4 million moved north and west, many poor African Americans were left behind. Black poverty rates in the South were the highest in the nation. While 18% of the black population lived in poverty in the rural South, the median was almost 25%, indicating that in more than half of the counties one fourth of the population was poor (Map 103).

Hispanics

In 1970, there were approximately 10 million Hispanics living in the United States. While distributed across the nation, poor Hispanics were concentrated in the West and in the mountain states (Map 104). Compared with African Americans, in 1970 the rate of poverty for Hispanics was quite low. This low rate in the early 1970s, which is derived from available census data, may be due to the definition of Hispanic as a racial/cultural group used in the 1970 enumeration.

Families

Family poverty in rural areas in 1970 mirrored the physical locations of the rural poor more generally. Rural poor households with children were concentrated in the U.S. South, Appalachia, the Carolina Piedmont, Indian reservations, and the borderlands between the U.S. and Mexico. The pattern of rural poverty location in 1970 changed little in subsequent decades (Map 105).

Female-headed households

Being a single-parent, female-headed household often meant relegation to a life of poverty. In 1970, the median rate of poverty in female-headed households in rural areas was significantly above that for all families. In almost half of rural female-headed households poverty was endemic. While such households were more spatially dispersed, female-headed households in rural areas appeared to fare better in the U.S. Midwest than in other regions of the nation (Map 106).

Rural Poverty in 2000

How much has the spatial distribution of rural poverty changed over the last thirty years?

By the beginning of the 21st century, rural America had declined in both the number of counties and percent of population. Many formerly rural counties of the South became suburbs to the region's major metropolitan areas. The once rural South had, by the beginning of the 21st century, begun to look more like the nation in terms of rates of urbanization.

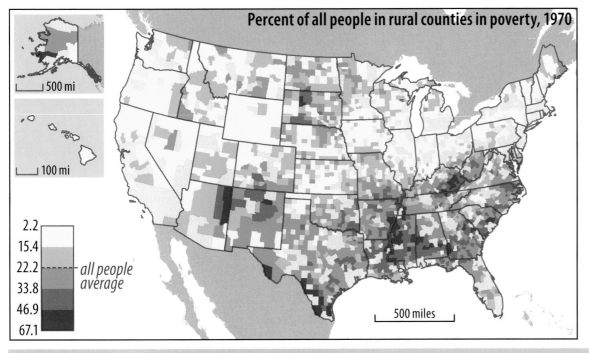

Map 100. *Rural poverty was prevalent in 1970*

Scale legend:
- 500 mi
- 100 mi

Percent of all people in rural counties in poverty, 1970

Legend values:
- 2.2
- 15.4
- 22.2 — *all people average*
- 33.8
- 46.9
- 67.1

500 miles

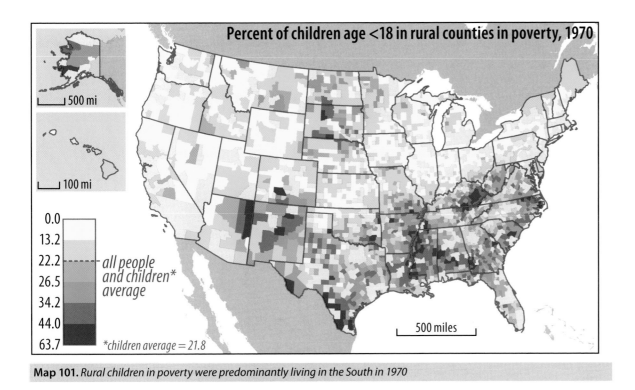

Map 101. *Rural children in poverty were predominantly living in the South in 1970*

Scale legend:
- 500 mi
- 100 mi

Percent of children age <18 in rural counties in poverty, 1970

Legend values:
- 0.0
- 13.2
- 22.2 — *all people and children* average*
- 26.5
- 34.2
- 44.0
- 63.7 *children average = 21.8*

500 miles

With urbanization and national economic growth, poverty rates declined over the 30-year period from 1970 to 2000. From a median rate of poverty of almost 19% in 1970, by 2003 the median poverty rate in rural counties had dropped to around 14% (Map 107). Poverty had moved to more remote regions of the country, including the upper Great Plains, the Atlantic Seaboard, and the Northern Sierra region of California. Still, the regions that were experiencing the most persistent rates of poverty included the Mississippi Delta, the U.S.–Mexico Border, the core counties of central Appalachia, and Native American Indian lands.

Vulnerable groups, including rural children, the elderly and people of color (particularly African Americans and Hispanics), and families especially female-headed households with children were geographically concentrated and demonstrated high rates of poverty compared with national averages (Figure 74) (Maps 108–111).

Summary

Despite more than forty years of policy designed to reduce rural poverty, the poor continue to find themselves concentrated in rural locations. The main reason for the persistence of rural poverty is the lack of economic opportunity. Of those counties that became urban over the intervening thirty years, many still boast high rates of poverty even as they exist within the shadow of some of the nation's largest urban areas (Map 112).

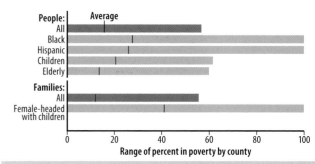

Chart axis labels:

People:
- All
- Black
- Hispanic
- Children
- Elderly

Families:
- All
- Female-headed with children

Average

0   20   40   60   80   100
Range of percent in poverty by county

Figure 74. *Summary of 2000 poverty statistics for each group in rural counties*

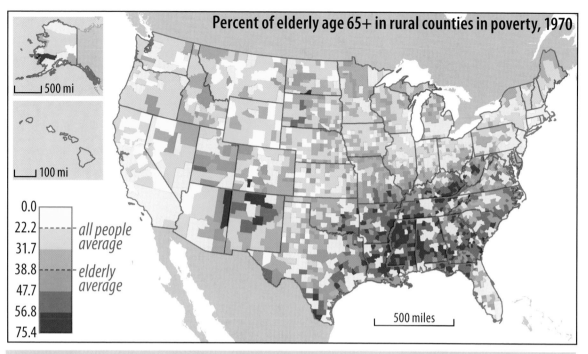

Percent of elderly age 65+ in rural counties in poverty, 1970

0.0	
22.2	*all people average*
31.7	
38.8	*elderly average*
47.7	
56.8	
75.4	

Map 102. *In 1970, the elderly poor escaped poverty in the industrial heartland*

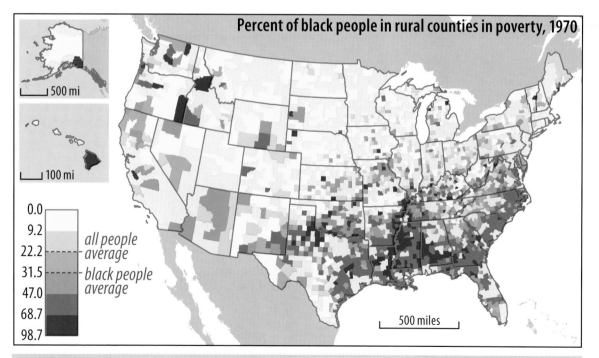

Percent of black people in rural counties in poverty, 1970

0.0	
9.2	
22.2	*all people average*
31.5	*black people average*
47.0	
68.7	
98.7	

Map 103. *Poverty was endemic to the South where African Americans predominantly lived*

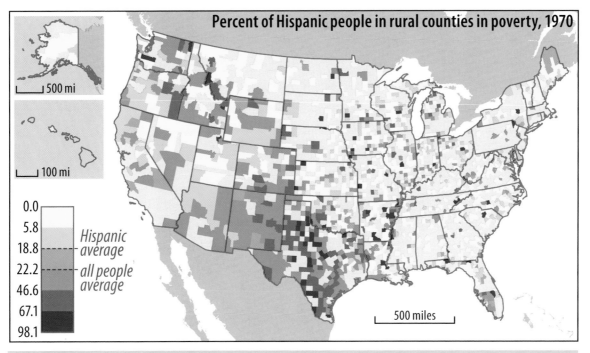

Percent of Hispanic people in rural counties in poverty, 1970

500 mi

100 mi

0.0
5.8
18.8 — *Hispanic average*
22.2 — *all people average*
46.6
67.1
98.1

500 miles

Map 104. *In 1970, poor Hispanics lived predominantly in the Southwest and InterMountain West*

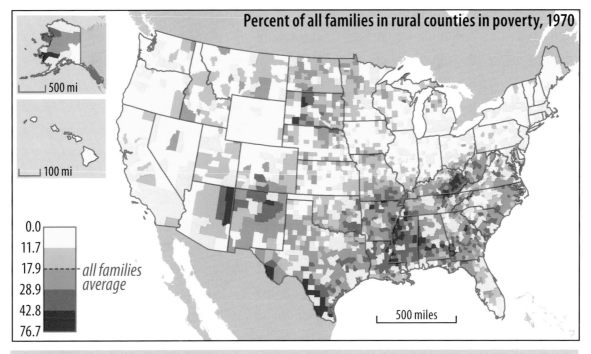

Percent of all families in rural counties in poverty, 1970

500 mi

100 mi

0.0
11.7
17.9 — *all families average*
28.9
42.8
76.7

500 miles

Map 105. *In 1970, poor families were mainly found in the nation's economically distressed regions*

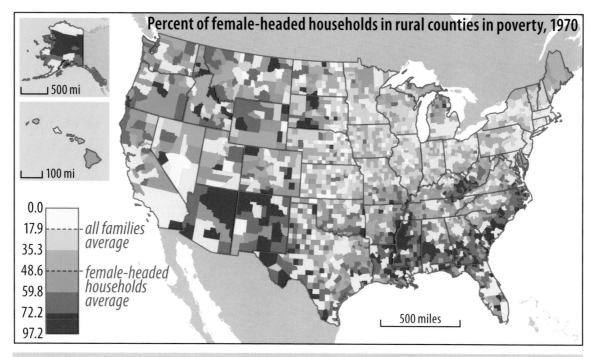

Percent of female-headed households in rural counties in poverty, 1970

500 mi

100 mi

0.0	
17.9	--- all families average
35.3	
48.6	--- female-headed households average
59.8	
72.2	
97.2	

500 miles

Map 106. *In 1970, female-headed households with children escaped poverty in the Industrial Northeast and Midwest*

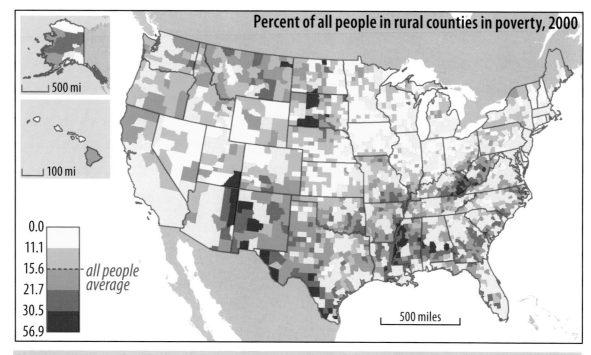

Percent of all people in rural counties in poverty, 2000

500 mi

100 mi

0.0	
11.1	
15.6	--- all people average
21.7	
30.5	
56.9	

500 miles

Map 107. *In 2000, rural poverty has become concentrated around urban areas of the South and West*

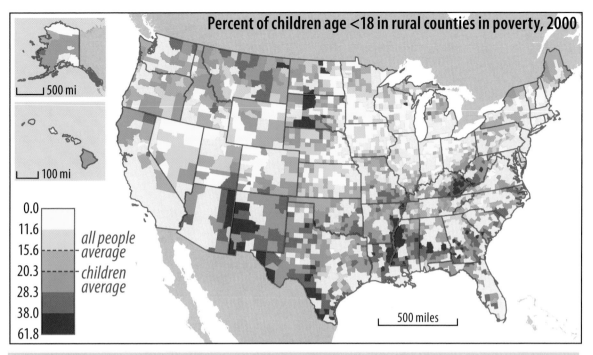

Percent of children age <18 in rural counties in poverty, 2000

0.0	
11.6	
15.6	*all people average*
20.3	*children average*
28.3	
38.0	
61.8	

500 mi

100 mi

500 miles

Map 108. *Child poverty in rural areas in 2000 was noticeably absent in the industrial heartland*

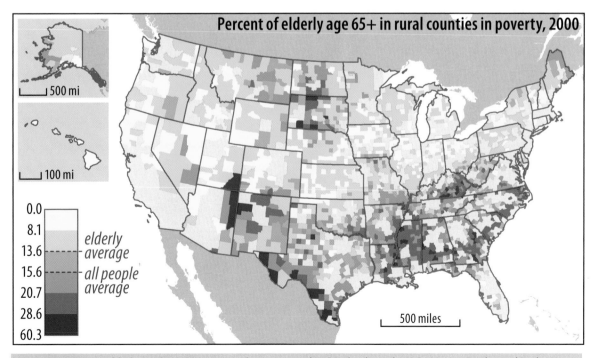

Percent of elderly age 65+ in rural counties in poverty, 2000

0.0	
8.1	
13.6	*elderly average*
15.6	*all people average*
20.7	
28.6	
60.3	

500 mi

100 mi

500 miles

Map 109. *In 2000, elderly rural poverty remained concentrated in South, along the U.S.–Mexico Border and in the Upper Midwest*

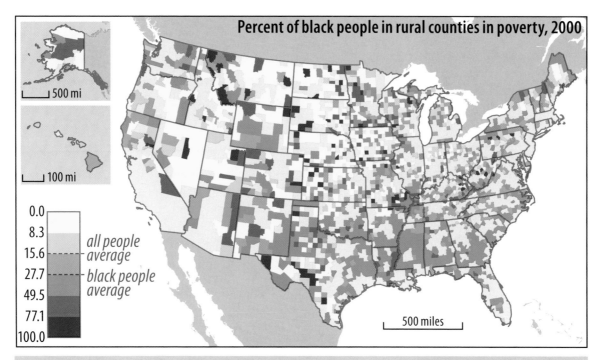

Percent of black people in rural counties in poverty, 2000

0.0
8.3
15.6 — all people average
27.7 — black people average
49.5
77.1
100.0

500 mi
100 mi
500 miles

Map 110. *Rural black poverty in 2000 encircled the nation's urban areas and remained concentrated in rural areas of the South*

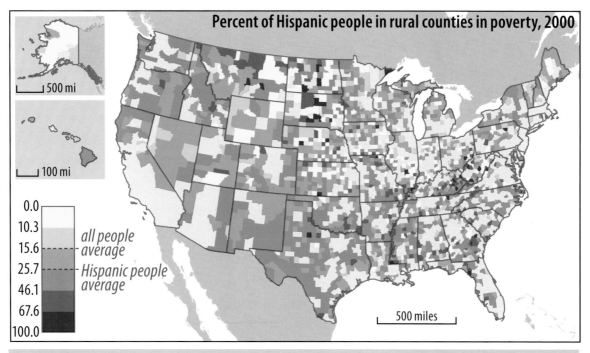

Percent of Hispanic people in rural counties in poverty, 2000

0.0
10.3
15.6 — all people average
25.7 — Hispanic people average
46.1
67.6
100.0

500 mi
100 mi
500 miles

Map 111. *In 2000, Hispanic poverty remained a southwestern and western phenomenon*

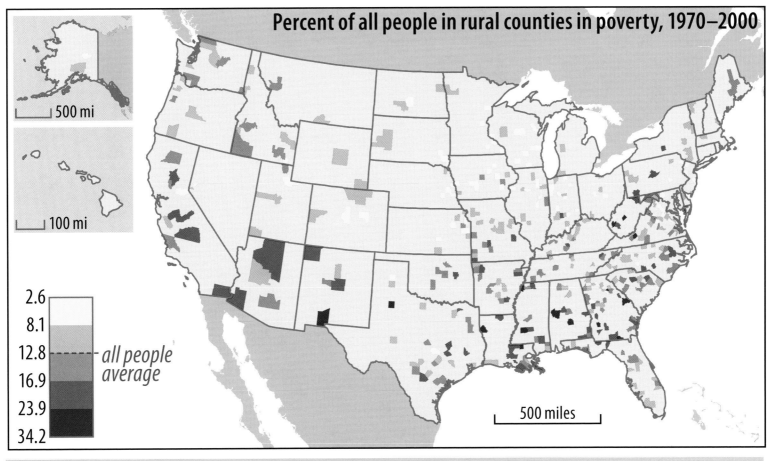

Percent of all people in rural counties in poverty, 1970–2000

500 mi

100 mi

2.6
8.1
12.8 ---- *all people average*
16.9
23.9
34.2

500 miles

Map 112. *Poverty rates remained high, particularly in southern counties that became urban during 1970–2000*

Segregation: *A Nation Spatially Divided*

Despite more than three decades of policy designed to increase integration, residential segregation by race/ethnicity and income has increased in U.S. metro areas since the 1970s. The belief that integration would reduce social stress and increase economic well-being has given way to the realization that America remains a nation divided by race and income.

To measure segregation, researchers calculate an index (Index of Dissimilarity [D]), which measures the degree to which two groups are evenly spread among census tracts or other geographic units in a given city. The Index of Dissimilarity ranges from 0 to 100; a score of 60 is considered high and indicates that 60% of either group must move to a different tract for the two groups to become more equally distributed. Values below 30 reflect low levels of segregation. Mapping the spatial distribution of metro areas with high and low concentrations of African Americans provides an initial perspective on the spatial distribution of urban Americans.

Patterns of Racial and Regional Segregation

Segregation levels are the most extreme between black and other populations, most notably white, followed by Asian and Hispanic (Map 113). Based on the Index of Dissimilarity, no other minority group experiences residential segregation to the same extent in the United States (Figure 75).

This means that whites live in neighborhoods predominantly with other whites and very infrequently live in neighbor-

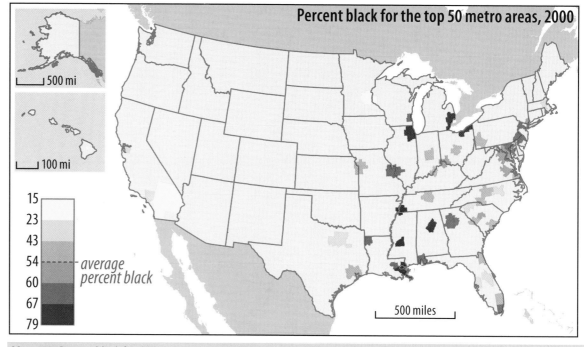

Map 113. *Percent black for the top 50 metro areas, 2000*

hoods with blacks. Moreover, from 1980–2000 few gains were made in terms of the integration of blacks and whites. The largest gains occurred in metro areas where the black population in 1980 was very small. In metro areas where blacks were more than 20% of the population, very little change occurred during these two decades (Figure 76).

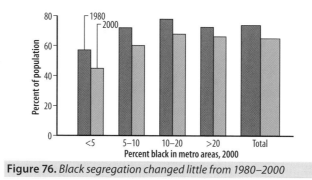

Figure 76. *Black segregation changed little from 1980–2000*

Mapping metro areas with high and low rates of blacks in the population reveals a very spatially skewed pattern of segregation. Poor blacks and poor whites also experience segregation in quite different ways. Poor whites tend to live in non-poor

neighborhoods whereas poor blacks tend to live in poor neighborhoods (Table 33).

White Poor	Black Poor
About 70% of poor non-Hispanic whites live in non-poor neighborhoods in the 10 largest cities in the central U.S.	16% of poor blacks live in non-poor neighborhoods in the 10 largest cities in the central U.S.
Less than 7% of whites live in extreme poverty or ghetto areas	38% of blacks live in extreme poverty or ghetto areas
In New York City, 70% of poor whites live in non-poverty neighborhoods	In New York City, 70% of poor blacks live in poverty neighborhoods
Poor whites, even those from broken homes, tend to live in communities with relatively stable families	The majority of poor blacks live in communities characterized by high rates of family disruption

Table 33. *Differences between white poor and black poor*

Percent Blacks versus Whites in Metro Areas, 2000

Persistent segregation is particularly evident in metro areas adjacent to the Great Lakes, including Cincinnati, Chicago, Cleveland, Detroit, and Milwaukee. Further, the most segregated cities in the United States have virtually remained the same as far back as the start of the 20th century (Table 34).

The Roots of Segregation

The existence of such persistent segregation in the Great Lakes region is best explained by the common histories of cities in

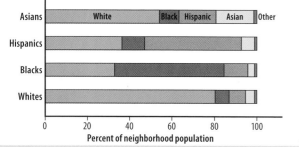

Figure 75. *Diversity experienced in each group's typical neighborhood, national median average*

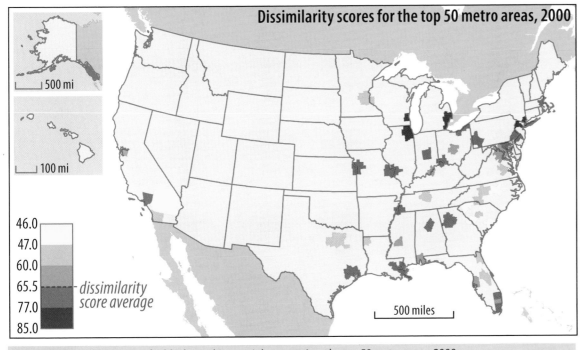

Dissimilarity scores for the top 50 metro areas, 2000

46.0	
47.0	
60.0	
65.5	*dissimilarity*
77.0	*score average*
85.0	

Map 114. *Dissimilarity scores for black vs. white spatial segregation, the top 50 metro areas, 2000*

Dissimilarity index for blacks vs. whites, top 10 cities in 2000, 1980–2000

2000 rank	Area name	Segregation		
		2000	1990	1980
1	Detroit, MI	85	88	88
2	Milwaukee-Waukesha, WI	82	83	84
3	New York, NY	82	82	82
4	Chicago, IL	81	84	88
5	Newark, NJ	80	83	83
6	Cleveland-Lorain-Elyria, OH	77	83	86
7	Cincinnati, OH-KY-IN	75	77	79
8	Nassau-Suffolk, NY	74	77	78
9	St. Louis, MO-IL	74	78	83
10	Miami, FL	74	73	81

Table 34. *Blacks and whites do not live in the same neighborhoods*

the region. Early 20th-century economic growth and demographic trends set the region apart from the rest of country. Residential and economic development in the Great Lakes region was most extensive at the start of the 20th century, coinciding with the nation's industrial boom.

During the following decades, the region attracted millions of black Southerners seeking employment. Initially, that population resided in economically and physically limited geographic spaces, but as incomes began to rise and open-housing laws were passed, blacks gradually migrated out of those neighborhoods. Yet despite increased prosperity, the residential segregation of blacks in the Great Lakes region persisted because as blacks made their entrance into more affluent neighborhoods, whites made their exit. This migration pattern accelerated during the Civil Rights Era, when Great Lakes metro areas were particularly hard-hit by racial rioting. The mass exodus of the white population that followed further intensified the extent of residential segregation by race/ethnicity and income, and the degree of social exclusion for the region's black population (Map 114). The situation is most grave for black children who, in cities like Detroit, Chicago, and Cleveland, are among the most segregated in the nation not only residentially, but more so scholastically.

Hispanic Segregation

Hispanics experience segregation in remarkably similar ways to those of African Americans in terms of geographic isolation from whites. As with blacks, cities with large Hispanic populations show low shares of whites in the population. Another measure of spatial segregation, the Index of Isolation, captures the extent to which a population group lives in census tracts where the majority of persons in the tract are of a particular race. The Index of Isolation indicates that in metro areas with large Hispanic populations, Hispanics tend to live in neighborhoods with very high concentrations of other Hispanics (Table 35).

Hispanic isolation, top 10 metro areas, 1980–2000

2000 rank	Area name	Value		
		2000	1990	1980
1	Laredo, TX	95	94	92
2	McAllen-Edinburg-Mission, TX	90	87	85
3	Brownsville-Harlingen-San Benito, TX	88	86	81
4	El Paso, TX	83	78	74
5	Miami, FL	71	68	59
6	Salinas, CA	68	59	49
7	Corpus Christi, TX	66	65	65
8	San Antonio, TX	66	65	66
9	Los Angeles-Long Beach, CA	63	58	50
10	Visalia-Tulare-Porterville, CA	61	51	42

Table 35. *The most segregated cities for Hispanics are in Texas*

There has been virtually no change in the segregation of Hispanics from 1980 to 2000 (Figure 77). In addition, like blacks, poor Hispanics tend to live in neighborhoods where other poor Hispanics are found.

Also like blacks, cities with large Hispanic populations tend to be geographically isolated from metro areas where there are large concentrations of whites (Map 115).

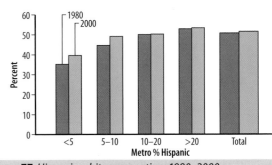

Figure 77. *Hispanic-white segregation, 1980–2000*

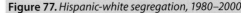

Cities with high levels of segregation among whites and Hispanics are found in the West and the Northeast (Table 36). Hispanics in the East have tended to migrate to the U.S. from the Dominican Republic and Puerto Rico, whereas Hispanics in the West have primarily migrated from Mexico and Latin America.

Dissimilarity index for Hispanics vs. whites, top 10 cities, 1980–2000

2000 rank	Area name	Segregation		
		2000	1990	1980
1	New York, NY	67	66	65
2	Newark, NJ	65	67	67
3	Los Angeles-Long Beach, CA	63	61	57
4	Chicago, IL	62	63	64
5	Philadelphia, PA-NJ	60	63	63
6	Salinas, CA	60	57	55
7	Boston, MA-NH	59	55	55
8	Bergen-Passaic, NJ	58	59	61
9	Ventura, CA	56	53	54
10	Orange County, CA	56	50	43

Table 36. *The top ten metro areas' dissimilarity index for Hispanics and whites*

The cost of segregation in relation to persistent poverty, particularly for the black-white and Hispanic-white population, is profound. The residential and educational distance between the groups fosters misconceptions and perpetuates racial stereotypes. Further, it serves to justify continued racial segregation and limits access to employment opportunities. Continued separation by race/ethnicity and income creates racially and socially homogenous public institutions that are geographically defined and politically polarized. In places like the Detroit metro area, the costs have been staggering. For generations poor blacks have faced depressed housing values and higher rates of crime and infant mortality than have whites, in addition to limited access to quality education and jobs. Important institutions such as public schools with high minority populations have less revenue to spend per pupil compared with predominantly white school districts, further compromising the opportunities of children of color. The social consequence of segregation has been great, limiting opportunities for economic groups to interact in meaningful ways through work, school, and community.

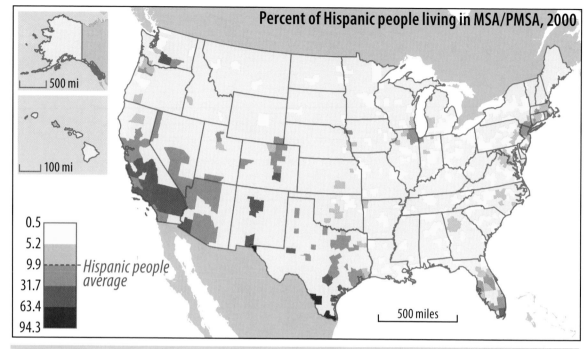

Percent of Hispanic people living in MSA/PMSA, 2000

500 mi

100 mi

0.5
5.2
9.9 — Hispanic people average
31.7
63.4
94.3

500 miles

Map 115. *Hispanic-white segregation, 1980–2000*

HISTORY OF POVERTY POLICY

1930s–2004

American Poverty Policy from the 1930s to 2004

From the 1930s to the 1950s

At the beginning of the 1960s, before the inauguration of the War on Poverty during the Johnson administration, federal programs to reduce poverty were based on social and economic issues that attended the national recovery from the Great Depression and the effects of World War II. Most, if not all, of the programs in place in the early 1960s were holdovers from the 1930s and 1940s.

Poverty policy in the 1930s and 1940s had several goals. These included the reduction of unemployment and the provision of partial income replacement with Social Security and family assistance, with the ultimate goal being to ensure the existence of a modest and short-term safety net for the poor. In 1946 Congress passed the Employment Act to avoid the high unemployment rates found after World War II. The Act committed the government to maintaining high employment and high levels of purchasing power. Given the buoyant economy after the war, there was little need for federal intervention and the Act went unimplemented. Concern for the poor remained latent through much of the 1950s with the exception of the extension of certain preexisting benefits to a larger group in society, including children and the elderly. It was not until the late 1950s, when the U.S. economy began to flag and persistent geographic pockets of poverty reemerged, that poverty again became a highly visible issue to both politicians and the public.

Early U.S. poverty policy sought to make the adjustments needed to ensure that all able-bodied persons with a job would be able to rise out of poverty and become contributing citizens of society. Existing poverty programs targeted the aged and certain family members such as women and children, but male workers were by and large excluded. This coverage, though well-intentioned and hard-fought, addressed only a small portion of the poverty problem. Lacking support were programs targeted toward individuals and families who worked but were still poor. In large sections of the nation, people worked but did not make a living wage (Levitan, 1973). In the South, mining and agriculture regions, and inner cities, work did not effectively pay (Douglas, 1971). Families with unemployed males present were most at risk. No programs addressed growing male under-employment, especially in conjunction with families. Programs worked against the nuclear family in which the father was unemployed. In some instances, public assistance programs actually encouraged the break-up of families.

In the absence of federal programs, states were expected to pick up the slack to some degree, but both state-level program variety and restrictions placed on eligibility proved even more discriminating and non-supportive of the working poor. Federal standards around social welfare were lax, allowing states great flexibility in the provision of programs and services. In-kind benefits, though more numerous and potentially enabling, required certain thresholds; thus, the poorest of the poor often failed to qualify for benefits. Overall, the biggest weakness of federal programs was attached to the underlying logic of "who was poor and why." From the 1930s through the 1950s, programs were shaped by the belief that people were employable and simply found themselves out of work. In this view, unemployment was purely transitory and thus the purpose of social programs, to the extent they were needed, was to provide for transitory unemployment. Unrecognized were the problems associated with geographic concentrations of poverty, poverty within nuclear families, poverty due to low incomes, and poverty associated with the working poor. However, race and gender did begin to emerge as issues in shaping poverty policy. This continued into the 1960s and beyond. As a result of unforeseen and largely disputed issues, by the 1960s the public consensus on poverty was that it was a national problem.

The 1960s

Discussions starting in the late 1950s recognized the place-based nature of poverty. In 1954, Senator Paul Douglas, campaigning in southern Illinois, learned first-hand about the acute needs of residents of his state who were living in poverty in the coal fields of the South. Profoundly moved by the abject poverty and recognizing that the problems were not a lack of employment but the conditions that made the state unattractive to economic activity, Douglas pressed for programs that addressed the nature of place-based poverty. He knew his state was not alone; moreover, he recognized that people in poor places were in many instances locked in, because human capital is far less mobile than financial capital. There was brief attention during the Eisenhower administration to the problem of place-based poverty, but the emphasis was on macro economics over more tailored programs for the poor. While a bill introduced in Congress in 1955 focused on the place-based nature of poverty, it would be another five years, many acrimonious fights, and several presidential vetoes before depressed area legislation passed and was signed into law by President Kennedy.

Aided by high post-war unemployment rates and Kennedy's campaign tour of Appalachia, after several false starts and intermittent efforts, two major programs were initiated: the Appalachian Redevelopment Authority and the Area Redevelopment Act. The Appalachian Redevelopment Authority brought to life the Appalachian Regional Commission (1965); the Area Redevelopment Act led to the creation of the Economic Development Administration (1965). Each was formulated to improve the economic potential of the nation's poorest areas. While the ARC had a defined geographic area in which to work, the EDA was responsible for essentially any place in the U.S. where unemployment was above the national average. Both programs emphasized the construction of infrastructure and in the case of the ARC, other areas of social capital development such as health care facilities.

Both defined the problem of economic distress as the result of high unemployment and the lack of economic conditions attractive to host capital. No mention was made of the working poor, the disabled, or those for whom the labor market provided no access. Once again the problem of the poor was viewed as the short-term dysfunction of the labor market.

No one has been able to pinpoint the trigger that led to public interest in and concern for the poor, although many different perspectives exist. Key studies of the late 1950s produced for Congress or initiated by individuals such as Michael Harrington were greeted with little fanfare. Academics and public organizations undertook inquiries into the problems of the poor, but there was no immediate public reaction to this evidence. It was not until the plight of the poor entered the public sphere through the media that members of Congress and the White House took notice. While on the campaign trail in 1960, then Senator Kennedy's fateful trip through Appalachia made some mark in identifying the problems of the poor in the U.S. In 1963, the nation took notice of the miserable conditions in which many Americans lived, ultimately leading to the first rounds of modern poverty policy, starting in the early 1960s.

By the mid-1960s, programs that had been developed to reduce poverty included social insurance expansion and an increase in the amount of support for recipients. The creation of the Office of Economic Opportunity and the allocation of $18 billion for need-based programs that included cash benefits, education, training, health, and in-kind goods such as food formed the basis of the "War on Poverty" launched by Lyndon Johnson in 1964.

In the 1960s, the nation set out to improve the well-being of those citizens who had failed to thrive in the post-war boom economy. There was recognition that the poor were located in disadvantaged regions and lacked the skills to compete in the national economy. A sluggish economy in the early 1960s led to a tax cut designed to stimulate the economy and to create more jobs (Haveman, 1977). The federal government knew, however, that simulating the economy would not in itself reduce long-term poverty. The next step was to reduce the skills gap through training programs and other programs designed to help enable youth to compete for employment. The federal government also established a lunch program for students and made more widely available public health care. Those without insurance now had access to community health services and other institutional forms.

Programs did not emerge seamlessly. Indeed, had it not been for the Civil Rights Movement and an activist Supreme Court, poverty programs may not have seen the light of day. But the persistent problem of black poverty and the "Negro question," as Sar Levitan noted, "...made it transparently clear that a disproportionate number of Negroes were to be found in the ranks of the unskilled, the unemployed and the poverty stricken" (Levitan, 1968, p. 15). The close relationship between economic and political discrimination was poignantly highlighted when President Kennedy commented in 1963 that "...there is little value in a Negro's obtaining the right to be admitted to the hotels and restaurants if he has no cash in his pocket and no job" (as cited in Levitan, 1973).

Kennedy's untimely death did not stop the momentum built up during 1962–1963. Two days after being sworn in to complete President Kennedy's unfinished term, President Johnson, when briefed about the poverty program, said, "That's my kind of program. It will help people. I want you to move full speed ahead on it" (Levitan, 1973, p. 18). The War on Poverty was born.

From the 1960s into the 1970s

From the mid-1960s through the mid-1970s, there was a concerted effort to address the perceived underlying problems of poverty in the nation. Five key areas of programs were developed: Manpower training (including the Job Corps), the Neighborhood Youth Corps, the Manpower Development and Training Act, Jobs, and WIN. Along with employment and training opportunities, long recognized educational deficiencies were tackled through programs such as Head Start, Upward Bound, Follow Through, Teach Corps, and Title I of the Aid to Education Act. Health care long out of reach for many of the nation's population, particularly the poor, was addressed through the creation of Neighborhood Health Centers and Medicaid to subsidize health care expenses for AFDC recipients and the "medically indigent." Finally, the Community Action Program was established to provide access to the political and institutional processes governing daily affairs and particularly those that represented services for the poor. Legal Aid Services was established to combat inequality and ensure access to fair treatment in civil society.

Three types of public programs existed or were introduced in the early 1960s: means-tested income transfers, social insurance, and targeted education and training programs (Table 37). Means-tested programs distribute money and other resources to people with demonstrable need who meet specific criteria, including being aged, a single mother with children, or disabled. These are and always have been a small fraction of all public spending for the poor (Figure 78). These programs trace their beginnings to the Social Security Act of 1935.

The second type of program far more broadly available and often referred to as programs for the middle class is social insurance—programs including Social Security, Medicare, and unemployment insurance. Social Security in particular was immediately successful in reducing poverty for 78% of the elderly by the late 1970s (Table 38). These programs are largely financed through payroll taxes and are primarily targeted to those who have already found work but for one reason or another are unable to work at certain points in their life-times. They have been recipients of and continue to receive the largest share of federal funds for social welfare programs.

The third type equalizes incomes of the future by enhancing individual capabilities through the provision of education

Costs of major public assistance and social insurance programs for the elderly, totally disabled, and all others, 1960–1980 (billions of constant 1980 dollars)

Program	1960	1970	1980
Programs for the elderly			
Social insurance			
Social Security, old age, & survivors	$29.2	$60.7	$104.7
Public employee & railroad retirement	9.7	21.9	44.3
Medicare[a]	0.0	16.8	29.1
Cash assistance			
Supplemental security income (& old age assistance)	$4.5	$4.0	$2.7
In-kind benefits			
Medicaid[a]	$0.0	$4.1	$8.7
Food stamps	0.0	0.2	0.5
Housing[b]	0.1	0.5	2.5
Programs for the totally disabled			
Social insurance			
Social Security disability[c]	$1.6	$6.5	$15.4
Medicare[d]	0.0	0.0	4.5
Cash assistance			
Supplemental security income (& aid to the disabled)	$0.7	$2.1	$5.0
In-kind benefits			
Medicaid[a]	$0.0	$2.2	$7.0
Programs for others			
Social insurance			
Unemployment insurance	$8.4	$9.3	$18.9
Workers' compensation	3.6	6.5	13.6
Cash assistance			
Aid to families with dependent children (AFDC)	$2.8	$10.3	$12.5
General assistance (GA)	0.9	1.3	1.4
In-kind benefits			
Medicaid[a]	$0.0	$3.7	$7.5
Food stamps	0.0	1.1	8.6
Housing[b]	0.4	1.0	4.7

[a]Began in 1966
[b]Estimates based on fraction of persons receiving housing assistance who are elderly (see U.S. Bureau of the Census, 1982)
[c]Began in 1956
[d]Extended to the disabled in 1974

Table 37. *Social Security makes up the bulk of public assistance payments*

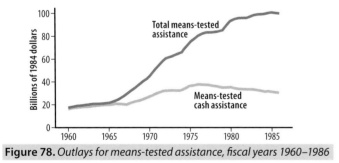

Figure 78. *Outlays for means-tested assistance, fiscal years 1960–1986*

and training. From 1968–1975, these programs helped lift thousands of Americans out of poverty. Their level of funding declined precipitously after 1978 (Figure 79). The impact of these different program designs on reductions of poverty can be seen from a variety of perspectives.

Percentage of pretransfer poor persons removed from poverty by cash transfers, by demographic group of household head and presence of children, 1965–1983

Demographic group	1965	1978	1983
Age <65			
White male, with children	12.3%	26.6%	20.6%
Nonwhite male, with children	7.0	22.9	13.3
White female, with children	30.1	21.8	13.8
Nonwhite female, with children	10.5	13.3	8.0
White, unrelated individuals & childless families	27.2	41.3	36.3
Nonwhite, unrelated individuals & childless families	11.7	28.1	24.5
Age 65+			
White	57.3%	78.5%	78.0%
Nonwhite	25.7	55.3	50.2
All persons in pretransfer poverty	26.8	43.6	37.1

Table 38. *Percent population moved out of poverty through federal programs*

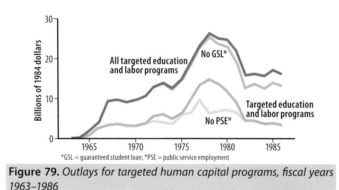

Figure 79. *Outlays for targeted human capital programs, fiscal years 1963–1986*

From 1960 to 1973 there was a quintupling of federal, state, and local spending on transfer programs to the poor. Over this period Aid to Families with Dependent Children rose significantly as both benefit levels rose and participation increased. Real spending increased in 1975–1976 to counter the effects of the 1974–1975 recession. From 1976 on, transfer payments to poor families declined significantly and failed due to a lack of price indexing to keep up with inflation over the 1976–1984 period. After 1960, spending on other cash assistance programs grew more slowly. Veteran benefits declined over that period. While outlays increased until the early 1970s for the blind and disabled, by the mid-1980s expenditures were flat. Reaching a peak in 1976, by the mid-1980s expenditures had fallen by 15% (Figure 80). Contrary to the rhetoric of the day, cash transfers rose by only 16% from 1971–1980, a figure that was significantly lower than the rate of inflation during that same time span.

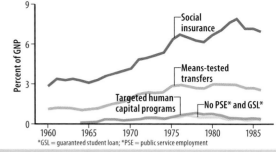

Figure 80. *Poverty-related spending as a percentage of Gross National Product, fiscal years 1960–1986*

A direct measure of the efficacy of poverty policy is something called "the poverty gap," which is the dollar amount needed to bring all poor households above the poverty line. The poverty gap is an effective means of expressing the amount of income people who are poor would have to make in addition to their existing earned income in order to be lifted out of poverty. Correlated with federal expenditures for poverty alleviation, the poverty gap provides a crude indication of the efficacy of public policy in reducing poverty among the nation's citizens. As seen in Table 39, from 1965 to 1979 the poverty gap closed somewhat as public policies designed to reduce poverty based on income, and in-kind and human capital augmenting investments, were put into effect. After 1980 the gap began to widen due to the national economic recession and the reduc-

Total poverty gap, 1965–1983 (billions of 1982 dollars)

Year	Official measure (1)	Adjusted measures (2)[a]	Adjusted measures (3)[b]	Adjusted measures (4)[c]	Pretransfer measure (5)
1965	$31.8	—	—	—	$ 67.6
1968	27.1	$19.2	—	—	65.1
1970	28.5	18.2	—	—	72.0
1972	27.9	12.3	—	—	78.3
1974	27.7	18.0	—	—	86.2
1976	28.3	—	—	—	92.9
1978	28.8	—	—	—	91.2
1979	30.8	—	$22.1	$17.9	92.1
1980	35.4	—	24.9	29.2	102.2
1981	40.1	—	29.1	23.7	108.4
1982	43.9	—	31.7	25.9	113.2
1983	45.6	—	—	—	116.2

[a]Based on recipient value of in-kind benefits but also corrected for underreporting and taxes
[b]Based on recipient value of in-kind benefits
[c]Based on market value of in-kind benefits

Table 39. *Percent additional income needed to move the poor above the poverty line*

tion in federal expenditures to relieve economic insecurity among the nation's most vulnerable populations. This measure tracked through time illustrates the declining fortunes of the nation's low-income groups.

The 1980s

Over that same time period, in-kind assistance programs experienced a dramatically different trajectory. Throughout the 1970s and into the early 1980s, in-kind transfers in the form of housing assistance, food stamps, subsidized school meals, and medical care rose strongly. The growth of these programs, though clearly tied to need, also met other national goals such as providing markets for agricultural surplus, jobs in cities for the construction and housing industries, and the cleaning up of so-called slums. Medical benefits were available to the poor, the disabled, and the aged.

Health care also experienced significant increases over the same time period, in part due to the enrollment of previously ineligible children and families. While comprising only 5% of means-tested programs in 1966, the figure rose to 30% in 1972 and to almost 40% in the mid-1980s. As Table 35 illustrated, federal spending for economic security had its largest impact in reducing poverty for the elderly. The reduced level of spending for families, children and the working poor starting in 1978 proved insufficient to stave off an increase in non-elderly poverty. As a way of summarizing the true meaning of public assistance through the mid-1980s, we can examine the fractions of $10 that went to the three types of programs. Approximately $3 of $10 in public assistance went to in-kind and means–tested programs for a total of $6. Only $3 of $10 were transferred as income. This was in sharp contrast to 1960 when $9 out of every $10 was transferred in the form of cash income that could be spent by the poor on goods and services as they saw fit. An explanation for this dramatic change refers to the public's growing preference for programs that were earmarked rather than discretionary. A secondary explanation was that as the economy became less able to generate high-paying jobs and incomes were eroded by Vietnam War era inflation, policy

makers were still able to push for public assistance programs if they were tied to social goals such as raising the incomes of farmers and ensuring jobs for the construction industry. Whatever the explanation, the result was a shift in the composition and effect of public expenditures to reduce poverty.

While public transfers as a fraction of national income nearly doubled from the early 1960s to the mid-1980s, the amount was actually quite modest and changed little after the mid-1970s. The benefits of both the income transfer and means-tested programs of the 1970s in reducing poverty during that period has been well documented. According to research at the time, approximately 84% of cash transfers and 73% of means-tested assistance went to families at or below the poverty line. Much of these expenditures went directly to reducing the poverty gap of the poor (the percentage of payments that actually alleviated officially measured poverty by subtracting that portion of monthly benefits that raised a family's income above the poverty line). Despite these efforts, the rate of poverty decline was modest. Thus, although resources were expended on behalf of the poor, these did not prove sufficient to bring the poverty rate down to expected levels. Research suggests the modest decline was due to several factors, including the high level of administrative costs associated with the poverty programs, and the lack of census-based reporting of transfer income that would tend to underestimate the relief provided by such transfers. Most importantly, a large fraction of all income-conditioned transfers went to the institutionalized elderly in the form of payments for Medicare.

Over the late 1970s and throughout the early 1980s, growing dissatisfaction was evident in the lack of progress in reducing poverty despite significant government investment in various programs. Two issues should be mentioned here. First, the amount of funding allocated for poverty reduction was never sufficient to reduce poverty to zero. As Table 35 illustrated, the vast bulk of expenditures for income security did not go to poor families, children, and the working poor. Indeed, the largest increases from 1960–1980 occurred in social insurance

programs, predominantly for the elderly and the disabled. Another large increase occurred in social insurance programs and unemployment. Over that same period, Cash Aid to Families with Dependent Children increased modestly, as did in-kind benefits. This level of funds was unable to halt the rise in poverty starting in the early 1980s (Table 40). Taken together, expenditures for the non-elderly were too small to reduce poverty significantly. In light of the facts regarding the level of

U.S. poverty under alternative income and threshold definitions, 1968–1998				
	Poverty population		Average income of poor (percentage of poverty line)	Poverty gap (percentage of GDP)
Year	Number (Millions)	Percentage of population		
Under official poverty definition				
1968	25.4	12.8%	60%	1.14%
1972	24.5	11.9	60	1.01
1976	25.0	11.8	60	0.96
1980	29.3	13.0	58	1.11
1984	33.7	14.4	56	1.19
1988	31.7	13.0	56	1.02
1992	38.0	14.8	55	1.18
1996	36.5	13.7	56	1.03
1998	34.5	12.7	54	0.96
Alternative poverty definition: Not accounting for medical spending				
1979	24.7	11.1%	64%	0.79%
1980	27.5	12.2	64	0.89
1981	30.7	13.5	64	0.97
1982	33.7	14.7	64	1.08
1983	35.5	15.3	64	1.08
1984	33.7	14.4	65	0.94
1985	33.1	14.0	65	0.91
1986	32.2	13.5	65	0.86
1987	32.3	13.4	65	0.84
1988	32.4	13.3	64	0.83
1989	32.0	13.0	64	0.79
1990	33.6	13.5	65	0.82
1991	35.2	14.0	64	0.88
1992	37.7	14.7	63	0.93
1993	39.2	15.1	62	0.99
1994	36.1	13.8	61	0.91
1995	33.8	12.8	64	0.79
1996	34.3	12.9	64	0.78
1997	33.6	12.5	62	0.79
1998	32.4	12.0	61	0.77
Alternative poverty definition: Subtracting medical spending from household income				
1990	44.3	17.8%	58%	1.32%
1991	46.2	18.4	58	1.40
1992	49.8	19.4	56	1.50
1993	51.6	19.9	54	1.60
1994	48.4	18.5	54	1.48
1995	46.7	17.7	56	1.34
1996	46.6	17.5	57	1.30
1997	45.9	17.1	55	1.29
1998	43.6	16.1	53	1.24

Table 40. *Average income of the poor as a percent of the poverty line*

expenditures made to reduce poverty and the change in them over time, by the early 1980s the public mood had changed dramatically. Many believed that public expenditures should be reined in because the federal government may not be in a position to win a war against economic insecurity.

The 1980s were marked by the coming to office of a president whose political agenda set forth a decade of defiant poverty policy, beginning with the intent to dismantle existing welfare programs and ending with a modest effort toward welfare reform. This policy movement reflected a unified frustration over the effectiveness of New Deal and War on Poverty programs in the aftermath of the 1970s and a difference of opinion between conservatives and liberals with respect to how the government could and should intervene to promote well-being. The result of this policy shift was a less than 1.5% rate of growth per annum in social welfare spending during the first Reagan administration, during a time when national unemployment levels broke records.

The conservative view was that past policy makers had failed to develop programs that appropriately addressed the inadequacies of the market economy and motivated individuals to work. Without recognizable incentives to work, those individuals had become dependent on state aid and families were suffering the consequences. In other words, there was little incentive for the poor to seek employment when the jobs for which most were qualified offered low wages and few benefits. Thus, together with the safety net provided by federal welfare programs for families and individuals, such as Aid to Families with Dependent Children (AFDC), food stamps, and Medicaid, there was little inclination to take advantage of existing work opportunities. Further, there was a loss of value on human capital development through education and work experience. The solution, therefore, was seen as the need to take away disincentives to work as represented by federal welfare programs for families and individuals such that the able-bodied would have little choice but to seek employment. Conjointly, many believed that the federal effort to foster a robust free market economy would lead to the trickling down of higher quality employment opportunities to the poor.

The harshness of the conservative approach produced heated debate through the mid-1980s. Much of this debate centered on appeals for welfare policy to uphold basic American values, such as individual autonomy, the importance of work, and the centrality of the family. This attitude ignored the fact that many of the poor did work, but did not make a living wage (Table 41) as seen in the share of income derived from market sources. Liberals and conservatives alike recognized that the health of the national economy was critical to the efficacy of federal poverty policy, noting that growth influences aspects of welfare dependency, such as the depth of poverty and associated family structure (e.g., female headship) (Table 42). Moreover, through the 1980s there was little evidence to support the argument that government programs were actually increasing the ranks of the poor because programs proved lucrative relative to getting a job. And, the age-old problem of discrimination in the labor market could not be ignored. Black males, especially black youth, were simply locked out of the labor market and therefore could not act freely to engage the American ideal of self-sufficiency as the better strategy for social welfare. Sufficient evidence existed to suggest that large numbers of the poor were working or would work if jobs were available. The lack of macro economic growth and

Sources of net income among people with income below the poverty threshold. Under alternative concepts of income, 1998			
Income concept or component of net income	Counting pre-tax market income (1)	Counting post-tax cash and near-cash income (2)	Subtracting out-of-pocket medical spending (3)
Market income	35	33	48
Taxes (except EITC)	-3	-3	-5
Social insurance	50	9	16
Means-tested transfers (including EITC)	22	22	20
Out-of-pocket medical spending	-18	-13	-25
Total income, ignoring medical spending[a]	104	61	78
Total income, subtracting medical spending	86	48	53
People below poverty threshold (millions)	57.6	32.4	43.6

[a]Post-tax, post-transfer income, including near-cash transfer benefits.

Note: Average income of each type is measured as a percentage of the poverty threshold. The poverty thresholds are derived from the Census Bureau's estimates of the food, clothing, and shelter consumption patterns of the median reference family, updated to 1998 using the CPI-U and the three-parameter equivalence scale (Short et al. 1999, C-2).

Table 41. *Sources of income for the poor*

Four decades of growth, cyclical swings, and the family poverty rate

Decadal patterns

Years	Percentage change in GDP growth per capita	Family poverty start	End	Change in poverty rate (percentage points)
1959–1969	34.6%	18.5%	9.7%	-8.8
1969–1979	23.8	9.7	9.2	-0.5
1979–1989	22.9	9.2	10.3	1.1
1989–1999	22.2	10.3	9.3	-1.0

Cyclical Patterns

	Change in unemployment rate	Change in poverty rate	Change in poverty rate / Change in unemployment rate
Recessions			
1959–1961	1.2	-0.4	—
1969–1971	2.4	0.3	0.13
1973–1975	3.6	0.9	0.25
1979–1982	3.9	3.0	0.77
1989–1992	2.2	1.6	0.73
Recoveries			
1961–1969	-3.2	-8.4	2.63
1971–1973	-1.0	-1.2	1.20
1975–1979	-2.3	-0.5	0.22
1982–1989	-4.4	-1.9	0.43
1992–1999	-3.3	-2.6	0.79

Table 42. *Unemployment and poverty levels are linked*

continued discrimination remained serious impediments to reducing further the ranks of the poor. The evidence, though voluminous, did not carry the day. The consensus was that a new approach was needed to win the war on poverty.

Data that track the poverty gap over twenty years—1979–1999—reveal that starting sometime in the early 1980s the poverty gap began to widen. By the late 1990s, the average income of the poor reached only 60% of the poverty line. That meant that families who had earned income made only slightly more than half of the poverty level of income (Table 40).

By the late 1980s there was agreement that not enough was being done to help families climb out of poverty. In response, it was proposed that the family should be the foundation of welfare policy, with aid to families tied to individual job training, the requirement that absent fathers provide child support, and other initiatives whose goal was to help families achieve economic independence. In 1988, the president signed into law the Family Support Act, which marked a fundamental change in the purview of the nation's welfare system.

The legislative intent was to place a greater emphasis on welfare strategies that helped to integrate the poor into the economic mainstream, thereby enabling them to rise out of poverty on their own accord. Its main focus was on expanding the public effort to increase the skills and educational levels of the poor through relatively low-cost initiatives. For instance, the Act required that single parents on AFDC, with children above age 3, either get a job or enroll in a job-training course at the expense of the state or federal government. In addition, transitional support was to be given to those participating in programs to upgrade their skills, such as transportation, child-care, and Medicaid benefits. Therefore, the success of the Act, was largely dependent on the strength of the economy and its ability to supply an adequate number of jobs that pay a living wage, the continuance of federal funding, and the commitment and innovation of states within the constructs of their job-training programs.

Inevitably, the effort had little effect on entrenched poverty, such as that found in urban areas with high concentrations of the poor and isolated areas of rural America, for a number of reasons but particularly due to the structure of the economy and changes in the political arena. For instance, the decade produced a burgeoning service economy with an unprecedented number of jobs. However, those jobs were characterized by part-time and temporary positions that paid relatively low wages in comparison to an eroding, unionized manufacturing sector that offered well-paying jobs and benefits for those with few skills and a limited education. Therefore, the economic expansion of the 1980s did not produce expected reductions in poverty largely because the decline in unemployment was offset by a decline in real wages among low-skill workers. Also, by the start of the new decade, with mounting forces of recession, the Act's programs were facing budget difficulties that escalated with impending military engagement in the Middle East. Thus, the extent to which the new direction of the nation's welfare programs could be successful in facilitating work opportunities for the poor within the private economy was limited given structural transformations in the economic and political spheres of engagement.

The 1990s

What was certain by the close of 1992 was the rapid growth in the number of the nation's working poor. Yet the new administration sought to shift social policy to "make work pay, strengthen child support enforcement, and work-oriented welfare." Clearly, the emphasis remained on the individual work ethic and family responsibility, but the liberal embodiment of that political agenda rang through with the envisioning of a sizable role for the federal government to play in promoting well-being. That role was to include initiatives to reward work, ensure health coverage, and provide job training, childcare, and community service employment opportunities, in addition to work-oriented welfare. Hence, the Clinton administration sought to adopt the pro-market orientation of the 1980s while marrying it with a traditional Democratic approach to social policy. This came with the recognition that the success and sustainability of programs like the Earned Income Tax Credit, the end of long-term welfare dependency, and the provision of child and health care benefits, were inextricably linked to work.

Opposition and controversy were once again an impediment to the proposed reforms, but by 1996 the necessary prescriptions for change were in hand. At that time the U.S. witnessed a remarkable political alignment between conservatives and liberals that was instrumental in passing and implementing the Personal Responsibility and Work Opportunity Reconciliation Act. One of the major changes stemming from the Act was the abolishment of AFDC. In its place the Temporary Assistance to Needy Families (TANF) program was established to offer block grants to states in place of matching funds. This gave states greater discretion in setting eligibility requirements. The Act also included the establishment of time limits (no more than sixty months over a lifetime) for individuals receiving TANF benefits. Other key components were the strengthening of state incentives to enhance welfare-to-work efforts and the reduction or abolishment of eligibility for public assistance among select populations, such as that for non-citizens, non-elderly adults without children, and the disabled.

This package of welfare program reforms was to become one of the most successful social policies in aid of the poor. By 1999, the nation saw record low unemployment and poverty rates, AFDC (TANF) caseloads reduced to half, and substantial increases in employment and income levels of single-mother families. However, it is difficult to credit fully the 1996 legislation with those measures of success. The main reason is that the Act was implemented during one of the strongest and longest economic expansions ever experienced in the nation, extending from 1993 to 2000 (Table 43). This expansion produced remarkable growth and low levels of unemployment accompanied by low inflation and budget surpluses. The

Poverty reduction in the 1990s boom			
	1992	1999	Change
Poverty of individuals			
All	14.8%	11.8%	-3.0%
White	11.9	9.8	-2.1
Black	33.4	23.6	-9.8
Hispanic	29.6	22.8	-8.6
Age			
<18	22.3	16.9	-5.4
18–64	11.9	10.0	-1.9
65+	12.9	9.7	-3.2
Poverty of families			
All	11.9	9.3	-2.6
With children age <18	18.0	13.8	-4.2
Married	8.3	6.3	-2.0
Single female parent	47.1	35.7	-11.4
White	9.1	7.3	-1.8
With children age <18	14.0	10.8	-3.2
Married	7.8	5.9	-1.9
Single female parent	28.5	22.5	-6.0
Black	31.1	21.9	-9.2
With children age <18	39.1	28.9	-10.2
Married	15.4	8.6	-6.4
Single female parent	57.4	46.1	-11.3
Hispanic	26.7	20.2	-6.5
With children age <18	32.9	25.0	-7.9
Married	22.9	16.8	-6.1
Single female parent	57.7	46.6	-11.1

Table 43. *The boom of the 1990s benefited the poor*

economic boom was not fueled by expansionary government policy, but rather by private-sector spending and employment. Added to that was the fact that over the course of the 1990s the minimum wage went up four times and in tandem with increases in the Earned Income Tax Credit, which provides wage subsidies to low-income workers. Further, other programs in aid of the poor matured, such as Medicaid, food stamps, childcare, and the child tax credit. As such, the expectation would be falling poverty rates, decreasing caseloads, and expanding workforce participation rates at the close of the 1990s in the absence of the 1996 legislation. No doubt, the welfare reforms that took place from the late 1980s to the late 1990s represented a fundamental change in the political debate regarding the poor. The tremendous growth of the 1990s was unable to make major changes in the poverty experience of many individuals, those disabled, with low levels of education and those facing labor market discrimination (Table 44). Most importantly, 42% of persons considered poor in 1999 worked and were still living in poverty. The economic boom while generating jobs proved insufficient in magnitude and structure to change the fates of the truly poor.

Individuals age 16+ in poverty, 1999	
Characteristics	Percentage
Worked in 1999	42.1%
Did not work in 1999	57.9
Did not work because disabled	23.9
Did not work because retired	26.9
Did not work because of family obligations	23.4
Disabled	21.0
Age >64	15.0
Eight years of schooling or less	17.5
Nine to eleven years of schooling	26.7
Immigrant	24.9
Has at least one "risk" factor (disabled; age >64; eight years of schooling or less; or immigrant)	53.2

Table 44. *Work and people in poverty, 1999*

What has the current evolution in poverty policy brought about in terms of the welfare of the nation's most vulnerable citizens? The prospect is not bright. Recent evidence on the poverty gap and changes in the resources available to the poor, especially single-parent households with children, sug-

gests a dramatic decline in the welfare of the poor. Examining the poverty gap over the peak to peak business cycle years of 1979 to 1999, using Census Current Population Survey data, James Ziliak has demonstrated the occurrence of dramatic changes in the level and sources of income maintenance programs filling the poverty gap.

Over the two-decade time period, three trends are evident. First, over the 1979–1999 period social insurance increased by 7% as a fraction of GNP, largely as a result of the growth in the elderly and retirement populations and expenditures for Social Security and Medicare. Workmen's compensation and Social Security disability insurance also increased significantly over the same time period. Second, the decline in AFDC and its replacement with TANF payments resulted in an almost 50% decline in real expenditures for families formerly receiving income support payments (Table 45). Over time, with the decline in AFDC, families replaced these cash transfers with disability insurance support. This trend toward replacement was not consistent across groups in society, however. The most successful transfers occurred in married households,

Expenditures on selected income maintenance programs and revenues from income taxes, 1979–1999 (billions of 1999 dollars)			
	1979	1989	1999
Social insurance	$355.9	$504.7	$683.9
(Percent of Real GDP)	(6.9)	(7.3)	(7.4)
OASI	207.8	279.5	334.4
Medicare	66.9	129.7	233.4
Unemployment insurance	22.6	18.7	21.4
Workers compensation[a]	27.2	46.1	43.4
Disability insurance	31.4	30.7	51.3
Means-tested transfers	$115.6	$159.7	$276.2
(Percent of real GDP)	(2.3)	(2.3)	(3.0)
Medicaid	49.9	82.3	189.5
Supplement security	16.2	19.8	29.8
AFDC/TANF	24.7	23.2	13.5
Food stamps	14.9	15.7	15.8
Housing assistance	9.9	18.7	27.6
Individual income taxes	$893.3	$1201.3	$1663.6
(Percent of real GDP)	(17.4)	(17.4)	(17.9)
Federal	499.5	599.2	879.6
State	75.2	119.2	172.4
Payroll (FICA)	318.6	483.1	611.6
Earned income tax credit	4.7	8.9	31.9

[a]Due to missing data 1980 values of workers compensation are used for 1979.

Table 45. *Social insurance programs represent the bulk of public support for income maintenance*

leaving most poor families financially more vulnerable than in previous decades. In sum, the experiment of the 1990s to shift away from support of public welfare has resulted in a growth in income poverty that leaves the nation's most vulnerable members unprotected from economic uncertainty and insecurity.

Policy Today

In August 2004, the U.S. Bureau of the Census announced that poverty rates were up and income inequality was steady and at a post-war record level high. In December of the same year, the U.S. Bureau of Labor Statistics announced that 25% of all jobs in the U.S. economy did not pay a wage sufficient to raise a family of four above the poverty line. In some states as many as 30% of all jobs do not pay a living wage. America has become a nation of people where all able persons who can work, do, but many in doing so cannot make ends meet. Looming trade deficits, growing disparity in the availability of good jobs, reduced returns to investments in education, and the loss of labor-intensive manufacturing jobs in America's traditionally low-wage regions raise serious questions. America is not currently doing all it can to assist working families, those who are discriminated against in the labor market, and the disabled, to make ends meet. Is the U.S. about to return to a time when the invisible poor once again become visible for all to see?

Sources

Paradox

American Communities Project. browns4.dyndns.org/cen2000_s4/report. html

America's Second Harvest: The Nation's Food Bank Network. N.d. Fact Sheets: Current Poverty and Hunger Statistics. www.secondharvest. org/site_content.asp?s=59

Beale, Calvin. 2004. "Anatomy of Nonmetro High-Poverty Areas: Common in Plight, Distinctive in Nature". Amber Waves. USDA Economic Research Service. Washington DC.

Blodgett, Jeff. 2003. Manufacturing on the Ropes: A National Perspective. CT Business Magazine, July/August. www.cerc.com/detpages/services772.html

Bureau of Labor Statistics. 2002. A Profile of the Working Poor, 2000. Washington, DC: U.S. Department of Labor.

Caner, Asena, and Edward Wolff. 2003. Asset Poverty in the United States, 1984–1999: Evidence from the Panel Study of Income Dynamics. www. levy.org/default.asp?view=publications_view&pubID =fca3a440ee

Cole, R. G., et al. 2002. Statistical Analysis of Spatial Pattern: A Comparison of Grid and Hierarchical Sampling Approaches. Sage Urban Studies Abstracts, 30(2), pp. 143–275.

DeNavas-Walt, Carmen, Bernadette D. Proctor, and Robert J. Mills. 2004. U.S. Census Bureau, Current Population Reports, P60–226, Income, Poverty, and Health Insurance Coverage in the United States: 2003. Washington, DC: U.S. Government Printing Office.

Eberhardt M., D. Ingram, and D. Makuc. 2001. Urban and rural health chartbook. Health, United States, 2001. Hyattsville, MD: National Center for Health Statistics.

Fair Data. www.fairdata2000.com

Federal Financial Institutions Examination Council. www.ffiec.gov/default. htm

Fisher, Monica G., and Bruce A. Weber. 2004. Does Economic Vulnerability Depend on Place of Residence? Asset Poverty Across the Rural-Urban Continuum. RPRC Working Paper No. 04-01. Rural Poverty Research Institute.

Glasmeier, Amy. 2002. One Nation, Pulling Apart: The History of Poverty in the United States. Progress in Human Geography, 26(2), pp. 155–173.

Glasmeier, Amy and Tracey Farrigan. 2003. Poverty, Sustainability, and the Culture of Despair: The Utilization of Natural Assets in Support of Poverty Alleviation and Community Development in Appalachia. The Annals of the American Academy of Political and Social Science, 590, pp. 131–149.

Glasmeier, Amy, Lawrence Wood, and Kurt Fuellhart. 2003. Measuring Economic Distress: A Comparison of Designations and Measures. Southern Rural Development Center and ERS, U.S. Department of Agriculture.

Gledhill, J. 2002. "Disappearing the Poor?" A Critique of the New Wisdoms of Social Democracy in an Age of Globalization. Sage Urban Studies Abstracts, 30(1), pp. 3–139.

Greenstein, Robert and Isaac Shapiro. 2003. The New Definitive CBO Data on Income and Tax Trends. Center for Budget and Policy Priorities. www. centeronbudget.org/9-23-03tax.htm

HUD Environmental Maps/e-Maps. 198.102.62.140/emaps/searchframe.asp

Jolliffe, Dean. 2004. Nonmetro Poverty: Assessing the Effect of the 1990's, Amber Waves, U.S. Department of Agriculture, Vol. 1 Issue 4.

Lee, B., R. Oropesa, and J. Kanan. 1994. Neighborhood Context and Residential Mobility. Demography, 31(2), pp. 249–270.

Lichter, D., G. Johnston, and D. McLaughlin. 1994. Changing Linkages Between Work and Poverty in Rural America. Rural Sociology, 59(3), pp. 395–415.

Maskovsky, J. 2002. The Other War at Home: The Geopolitics of U.S. Poverty. Sage Urban Studies Abstracts, 30(1), pp. 3–139.

Mitlin, D. 2002. Civil Society and Urban Poverty: Examining Complexity. Sage Urban Studies Abstracts, 30(2), pp. 143–275.

Mosley, James M., and Kathleen Miller. 2004. What the Research Says About Spatial Variations in Factors Affecting Poverty. Research Brief 2004-1. Rural Poverty Research Institute.

Nord, Mark. 2003. Overcoming Persistent Poverty—And Sinking Into It: Income Trends in Persistent-Poverty and Other High-Poverty Rural Counties, 1989–1994. Rural Development Perspectives, Vol. 12 No. 3. www.ers.usda.gov/publications/rdp/rdp697/rdp697a.pdf

Lewis Mumford Center for Comparative Urban and Regional Research. mumford1.dyndns.org/cen2000/

O'Connor, Alice. 2000. Poverty Research and Policy for the Post-Welfare Era. Annual Review of Sociology, 26, pp. 547–562.

O'Hare, W. P. 1996. A New Look at Poverty in America. Population Bulletin, 51, pp. 1–48.

Reardon, Sean, and David O' Sullivan. 2004. Measures of Spatial Segregation. Penn State Working Paper.

Rich, M. J., M. W. Giles, and E. Stern. 2002. Collaborating to Reduce Poverty: Views from City Halls and Community-based Organizations. Sage Urban Studies Abstracts, 30(2), pp. 143–275.

Rural Policy Research Institute. www.rupri.org/centers/circ.asp

Tarmann, Allison, 2003. Fifty Years of Demographic Change in Rural America. Population Reference Bureau. www.prb.org/rfdcenter/50yearsofchange.htm

Tickamyer, Ann. Barry Tadlock, Julie White, and Debra Henderson. 2000. Where All the Counties Are Above Average: Top Down Versus Bottom Up Perspectives on Welfare Reform, Ohio University Welfare Reform Project.

Tienda, M. 1991. Poor People and Poor Places: Deciphering Neighborhood Effects on Poverty Outcomes. In J. Huber (ed.), Macro-Micro Linkages in Sociology. Newbury Park: Sage, pp. 244–261.

Understanding Poverty: Conference proceedings. Published in FOCUS, University of Wisconsin, Madison, Institute for Research on Poverty, 2000.

U.S. Bureau of the Census, Current Population Survey, www.census.gov/hhes/poverty

U.S. Bureau of the Census, Current Population Survey, 2004 Annual Social and Economic Supplement. Washington, DC: Author.

U.S. Bureau of the Census, Current Population Survey, 1960 to 2004 Annual Social and Economic Supplement. Washington, DC: Author.

U.S. Bureau of the Census, Current Population Survey, Annual Social and Economic Supplement. Washington, DC: Author.

U.S. Bureau of the Census, Historical Poverty Tables, at www.census.gov/hhes/poverty/histpov/hstpov4.html

Urban Poverty. www.urbanpoverty.net

Children

Annie E. Casey Foundation. 2004. Kids Count 2004 Data Book online. www. aecf.org/kidscount/databook

Catholic Campaign for Human Development. One Nation Free from Poverty. www.usccb.org/cchd/povertyusa

Centers for Disease Control and Prevention. 2003. Summary Health Statistics for U.S. Children: National Health Interview Survey, 2001. Vital and Health Statistics, Series 10, Number 216. Washington, DC: U.S. Department of Health and Human Services.

Children's Defense Fund. The State of Children in America's Union, A 2002 Action Guide to Leave No Child Behind. www.childrensdefense.org

Children's Defense Fund. 2003. 2002 Facts on Child Poverty in America. Online on the Children's Defense Fund web site at: www.childrensdefense.org/familyincome/childpoverty/basicfacts.asp

CLIKS: County-City-Community Level Information on Kids. www//aecf. org/cgi-bin/cliks.cgi

Eberhardt M., D. Ingram, and D. Makuc. 2001. Urban and rural health chartbook. Health, United States, 2001. Hyattsville, MD: National Center for Health Statistics.

Fair Data. www.fairdata2000.com

Harris, Rosalind and Julie Zimmerman. 2003. Children and Poverty in the Rural South. SRDC Policy Series. Economic and Workforce Development Nov., No 2. www.ers.usda.gov/AmberWaves/november03/Findings/childpoverty.htm

Hearts & Minds, Information for Change. n.d. Children in Poverty: America's Ongoing War. Online at: www.heartsandminds.org/articles/childpov. htm

Lewis Mumford Center for Comparative Urban and Regional Research. mumford1.dyndns.org/cen2000/

Lichter, D. 1997. Poverty and Inequality among Children. Annual Review of Sociology, 23, pp. 121–145.

Maternal and Child Health Bureau. 1998. Child Health USA. Washington, DC: U.S. Department of Health and Human Services.

Mosley, Jane, Kathleen Miller, and Heather Koball, 2003. Material Hardship Among Families and Children. Rural Policy Research Institute (RUPRI). University of Missouri. www.rupri.org/ruralPolicy/presentations/memphis3.pdf

National Center for Children in Poverty. Geography of Low-Income Children and Families. 2003. Columbia University. Mailman School of Public Health. Nov. www.nccp.org/media/gfs03-text.pdf

National Center for Education Statistics. nces.ed.gov/surveys/sdds, School District Demographics

National Center for Education Statistics. 2002. Public High School Dropouts and Completers from the Common Core of Data: School Year 2000–2001. Washington, DC.

National Center for Education Statistics. 2002. The Condition of Education 2002 in Brief. Washington, DC: Author.

National Center for Health Statistics. 2001–2003 National Immunization Survey. Washington, DC: Author.

O'Hare, William and Kenneth Johnston. 2004. Child Poverty in Rural America. Population Reference Bureau. Reports on America, 4(1).

O'Regan, Katherine, and John Quigley. 1996. Teenage Employment and the Spatial Isolation of Minority and Poverty Households. Journal of Human Resources, 31(3), pp. 692–702.

Pollard, Kelvin and Mark Mather. 2003. A 50-Year Decline in the Child Population in Rural Areas, Population Reference Bureau. www.prb. org/rfdcenter/50yeardecline.htm

Research Forum at the National Center for Children in Poverty. www. researchforum.org

Rogers, Carolyn. 2003. "Dimensions of Child Poverty in Rural Areas". Amber Waves, USDA. Nov.

Sampson, R. J. 1997. The Embeddedness of Child and Adolescent Development: A Community-Level Perspective on Urban Violence. In J. McCord, ed., Violence and Childhood in the Inner City. New York: Cambridge University Press, pp. 61–64.

Sherman, A. 1999. Children's Poverty in America. Forum for Applied Research and Public Policy, 14(4), pp. 68–73.

Swanson, Christopher. 2002. Who Graduates? Who Doesn't? A Statistical Portrait of Public High School Graduation, Class of 2001. Education Policy Center, The Urban Institute.

U.S. Bureau of the Census, Historical Poverty Tables, www.census.gov/hhes/poverty/histpov/hstpov4.html

U.S. Bureau of the Census, Current Population Survey, www.census.gov/hhes/poverty

U.S. Bureau of the Census, Current Population Survey, 1960–2004 Annual Social and Economic Supplements

U.S. Bureau of the Census. 2002. KIDS COUNT/PRB Report on Census 2000. Washington, DC: Author.

Urban Institute. 2005. Assessing the New Federalism: National Survey of America's Families: Many Young Children Spend Long Hours in Child Care. Research Forum Newsletter, National Center for Children in Poverty. www.researchforum.org

Women

Bianchi, S. 1999. Feminization and Juvenilization of Poverty: Trends, Relative Risks, Causes, and Consequences. Annual Review of Sociology, 25, pp. 307–333.

Browne, I. 2000. Opportunities Lost? Race, Industrial Restructuring, and Employment Among Young Women Heading Households. Social Forces, 78(3), pp. 907–929.

Centers for Disease Control and Prevention. Division of HIVAIDS Prevention. 1999. HIVAIDS surveillance report; 1999 year end report. Atlanta: Centers for Disease Control and Prevention; 11(2).

Dodoo, F., and P. Kasari. 1995. Race and Female Occupational Location in America. Journal of Black Studies, 25, pp. 465–474.

Eberhardt M., D. Ingram, and D. Makuc. 2001. Urban and Rural Health Chartbook. Health, United States, 2001. Hyattsville, MD: National Center for Health Statistics.

Fair Data. www.fairdata2000.com

Fishman, Mike. 2004. Multiple Work Supports and Services May Help Low-Wage Workers Climb the Economic Ladder. Research Forum Newsletter, National Center for Children in Poverty. www.researchforum.org

HUD Environmental Maps/e-Maps. 198.102.62.140/emaps/searchframe.asp

Institute for Women's Policy Research. 1999. Equal Pay for Working Families: A National Overview.

Institute for Women's Policy Research. 2004. The Status of Women in the States, 2004, www.iwpr.org/states2002/tables/table09.pdf

Institute for Women's Policy Research. 1995. How Women Can Earn a Living Wage.

Institute for Women's Policy Research. 1999. Network News.

Henry J. Kaiser Family Foundation estimates based on Urban Institute analyses of the March 1999 Current Population Survey, U.S. Bureau of the Census.

Mandell, B. 1996. Women and Welfare, Part One. NWSA Journal, 8, pp. 107–116.

Maternal and Child Health Bureau. 1998. Child Health USA. Washington, DC: U.S. Department of Health and Human Services.

Mathematica Policy Research. 2005. Building Strong Families Evaluation: Brief #3: What We Know About Unmarried Parents: Implications for Building Strong Families Programs. Research Forum Newsletter, National Center for Children in Poverty. www.researchforum.org

National Committee on Pay Equity. 1999. Newsnotes.

National Committee on Pay Equity. 1999.The Wage Gap: 1998.

National Committee on Pay Equity. 1999. The Wage Gap by Education: 1998.

National Committee on Pay Equity. 1999. The Wage Gap Over Time.

U.S. Bureau of the Census, Current Population Survey, 1961 to 2004 Annual Social and Economic Supplements.

U.S. Bureau of the Census. 1998. Current Populations Report. P60–206.

U.S. Bureau of the Census, Current Population Survey, www.census.gov/hhes/poverty

U.S. Bureau of the Census, Historical Poverty Tables, www.census.gov/hhes/poverty/histpov/hstpov4.html

Weber, Bruce, Mark Edwards and Greg Duncan. 2003. Single Mother Work and Poverty Under Welfare Reform: Are Policy Impacts Different in Rural Areas? Working Paper Series 03-7. University of Michigan, National Poverty Center.

Whitener, Leslie A., Robert Gibbs, and Lorin Kusmin. 2003. Rural Welfare Reform: Lessons Learned, Amber Waves, U.S. Department of Agriculture, Economic Research Service, Washington DC.

Blacks

The Black Population in the United States. March 1999. Current Population Reports, U.S. Bureau of the Census.

Bradbury, Katherine. 1999. How much do Expansions Reduce the Black-White Unemployment Gap?

Bureau of Justice Statistics Correctional Surveys; Correctional Populations in the United States 1997, Prison and Jail Inmates at Midyear and Census of Jails 1999, www.prisonpolicy.org/atlas/index.shtml

Bureau of Justice Statistics Correctional Surveys (The National Probation Data Survey, National Prisoner Statistics, Survey of Jails, and The National Parole Data Survey) as presented in Correctional Populations in the United States, 1997, Prison and Jail Inmates at Midyear and Census of Jails 1999.

Cancer Mortality Maps and Graphs Web Site, a service of the National Cancer Institute, www3.cancer.gov/atlasplus/charts.html

Carey, Kevin. 2003. The Funding Gap: Low-Income and Minority Students Still Receive Fewer Dollars in Most States. Washington, DC: The Education Trust.

Cohen, P. 1998. Black Concentration Effects on Black-White and Gender Inequality: Multilevel Analysis for U.S. Metropolitan Areas. Social Forces, 77(1), pp. 207–229.

Eberhardt M., D. Ingram, and D. Makuc. 2001. Urban and rural health chartbook. Health, United States, 2001. Hyattsville, MD: National Center for Health Statistics.

Fair Data. www.fairdata2000.com

Fishman, Mike. 2004. Multiple Work Supports and Services May Help Low-Wage Workers Climb the Economic Ladder. Research Forum Newsletter, National Center for Children in Poverty. www.researchforum.org

Gilens, M. 1996. Race and Poverty in America: Public Misperceptions and the American News Media. Public Opinion Quarterly, 60, pp. 515–541.

Glasmeier, Amy and Tracey Farrigan. 2005. The Economic Impacts of the Prison Development Boom on Persistently Poor Rural Places. International Journal of Regional Science. Under review.

Harrison, Paige M. and Allen J. Beck. 2004). Prisoners in 2003 (NCJ-205335). Bureau of Justice Statistics, U.S. Department of Justice. www.ojp.usdoj.gov/bjs/pub/press/p03pr.htm

Holzer, Harry, and Paul Offner. 2001. Trends in Employment Outcomes of Young Black Men. Paper from Extending Opportunities Project, National Center for Strategic Nonprofit Planning and Community Leadership, Charles Stewart Mott Foundation.

HUD Environmental Maps/e-Maps. 198.102.62.140/emaps/searchframe.asp

Joint Center for Political and Economic Studies. www.jointcenter.org

National Prisoners Statistics. 1997. Surveys of Inmates in State and Federal Correctional Facilities.

Mathematica Policy Research. 2005. Building Strong Families Evaluation: Brief #3: What We Know About Unmarried Parents: Implications for Building Strong Families Programs. Research Forum Newsletter, National Center for Children in Poverty. www.researchforum.org

National Archive of Criminal Justice Data, National Prisoners Statistics; Surveys of Inmates in State and Federal Correctional Facilities, 1997, www.icpsr.umich.edu/NACJD/SISFCF/

National Urban League. 2004. African-American Employment and Job Quality: Income, Wealth, and Health Insurance Benefits (Third Quarter 2004). Washington, DC: National Urban League Institute for Opportunity and Equality. QJR-04-2004.

Pattilio-McCoy, Mary. 1999. Middle Class, Yet Black: A Review Essay. Online at www.rcgd.isr.umich.edu/prba/perspectives/fall1999/mpattillo.pdf

Prison Policy Initiative, Online Atlas, Northampton, MA, www.prisonpolicy.org/atlas/index.shtml

Rankin, B., and J. Quane. 2000. Neighborhood Poverty and the Social Isolation of Inner-City African American Families. Social Forces, 79(1), pp. 139–164.

U.S. Bureau of the Census. Census 2000

U.S. Bureau of the Census Current Population Survey 1999

U.S. Bureau of the Census Historical Income Tables, www.census.gov/hhes/income/histinc/incperdet.html

U.S. Bureau of the Census, Statistical Brief. 1993. Black Americans, A Profile. www.census.gov/apsd/www/statbrief/sb93_2.pdf

U.S. Bureau of Labor Statistics, www.bls.gov/lau/home.htm

U.S. Department of Justice, U.S. Bureau of Justice Statistics, Census of Jails 1999, www.ojp.usdoj.gov/bjs/abstract/cj99.htm

U.S. Department of Justice, U.S. Bureau of Justice Statistics, Correctional Populations in the United States, 1997, www.ojp.usdoj.gov/bjs/abstract/cpus97.htm

U.S. Department of Justice, U.S. Bureau of Justice Statistics, Correctional Surveys (The National Probation Data Survey, National Prisoner Statistics, Survey of Jails, and the National Parole Data Survey).

U.S. Department of Justice, U.S. Bureau of Justice Statistics, Prison and Jail Inmates at Midyear, 2004, www.ojp.usdoj.gov/bjs/pubalp2.htm#pjmidyear

Hispanics

Gibson, Campbell, and Kay Jung. 2002. Historical Census Statistics on Population Totals By Race, 1790 to 1990, and By Hispanic Origin, 1970 to 1990, for The United States, Regions, Divisions, and States. Working Paper Series No. 56. Population Division, U.S. Census Bureau, Washington, DC 20233. www.census.gov/population/www/documentation/twps0056.html#gd

Kandel, William, and John Cromartie. 2004. New Patterns of Hispanic Settlement in Rural America. Rural Development Research Report No. RDRR99. 49 pp. (May). www.ers.usda.gov/publications/rdrr99/

Kochhar. R. 2004. The Wealth of Hispanic Households, 1996–2002. Washington, DC: Pew Hispanic Center Report.

Pew Charitable Trusts. 2005. A People in Motion. A Pew Center Research Program. pewresearch.org/trends/trends2005-hispanic.pdf

Elderly

Administration on Aging. 2004. A Profile of Older Americans. Washington, DC: U.S. Department of Health and Human Services.

AARP. 2002. Beyond 50: A Report to the Nation on Economic Security. Social Security Administration. Income of the Aged Chart Book 2001. Washington, DC: Policy Research Division, AARP.

AARP. n.d. Money Matters: How Economic Security Varies by Income. Washington, DC: Author.

AARP Public Policy Institute. 2004. Poverty Using Official and Experimental Measures. research.aarp.org/econ/ib66_poverty.pdf

Center for Budget and Policy Priorities. 1999. Strengths of the Safety Net: How the ETIC, SS, and Other Government Programs Affect Poverty.

Eberhardt M., D. Ingram, and D. Makuc. 2001. Urban and Rural Health Chartbook. Health, United States, 2001. Hyattsville, MD: National Center for Health Statistics.

Fair Data. www.fairdata2000.com

Federal Interagency Forum on Age-related Statistics. Older Americans 2000: Key Indicators of Well-being. www.agingstats.gov/chartbook2000/default.htm

HUD Environmental Maps/e-Maps. 198.102.62.140/emaps/searchframe.asp

Rank, M. R., and T. A. Hirschl. 1999. Estimating the Proportion of Americans Ever Experiencing Poverty During Their Elderly Years. Journals of Gerontology, Series B, 54B(4), pp. S184–S193.

Social Security Administration. 2002. Income of the Aged Chartbook. Washington, DC: Office of Policy, Office of Research Evaluation and Statistics, Social Security Administration.

U.S. Bureau of the Census, Historical Poverty Tables www.census.gov/hhes/poverty/histpov/hstpov4.html

U.S. Bureau of the Census, January 2004 Census Internet Release

U.S. Bureau of the Census. 2003. 65+ in the United States. Current Population Reports, Special Studies, P23–190.

U.S. Bureau of the Census, March 2003. Current Population Survey.

U.S. Bureau of the Census and U.S. Bureau of Labor Statistics. 2001. Current Population Survey.

U.S. Library of Congress archives www.archives.gov/exhibit_hall/treasures_of_congress/Images/page_19/63a.html

Working But Poor

Appelbaum, Eileen, Annette Bernhardt, and Richard J. Murnane. 2003. Low-Wage America: How Employers Are Reshaping Opportunity in the Workplace. New York: Russell Sage Foundation.

Berube. Alan and Thacher Tiffany. 2004. The "State" of Low-Wage Workers: How the EITC Benefits Urban and Rural Communities in the 50 States, Center for Metropolitan Policy. Washington D.:Brookings Institution. www.brookings.edu/dybdocroot/es/urban/publications/20040203berube.pdf.

Colclough, G., and C. Tolbert. 1990. High Technology, Work, and Inequality in Southern Labor Markets. Work and Occupations, 17(1), pp. 3–29.

Cotter, D., J. Hermsen, and R. Vannerman. 1999. Systems of Gender, Race, and Class Inequality: Multilevel Analyses. Social Forces, 78(2), pp. 433–460.

Eberhardt M., D. Ingram, and D. Makuc. 2001. Urban and Rural Health Chartbook. Health, United States, 2001. Hyattsville, MD: National Center for Health Statistics.

Glasmeier, Amy and Robin Leichenko. 1999. The Transformation of a Rural Region and the Rise of the New South: Miracle or Mirage? In Richard Tardinico (ed.), Poverty or Development? New York: Routledge, pp. 19–40.

Keister, Lisa A., and Stephanie Moller. 2000. Wealth Inequality in the United States. Annual Review of Sociology, 26, pp. 63–81.

Morris, Martina and Bruce Western. 1999. Inequality in Earnings in the United States. Annual Review of Sociology, 25, pp. 623–657.

Rector, Robert. 2004. Understanding Poverty and Economic Inequality in the United States. Backgrounder #1796. Online at the Heritage Foundation web site: www.heritage.org/Research/Welfare/bg1796.cfm

Tickamyer, A., and M. Latimer. 1993. A Multi-Level Analysis of Income Sources of the Poor and Near Poor. In J. Singelmann and F. Deseran (eds.), Inequalities in Labor Market Areas. Boulder: Westview, pp. 83–106.

U.S. Bureau of the Census. 1998. Current Populations Report. P60–206.

U.S. Bureau of the Census, Current Population Survey, www.census.gov/hhes/poverty

U.S. Bureau of the Census, Current Population Survey, 1960–2004 Annual Social and Economic Supplements

U.S. Bureau of the Census, Historical Poverty Tables www.census.gov/hhes/poverty/histpov/hstpov4.html

Wealthy Families

Eberhardt M., D. Ingram, and D. Makuc. 2001. Urban and Rural Health Chartbook. Health, United States, 2001. Hyattsville, MD: National Center for Health Statistics.

Gap Between Haves, Have-Nots Expands. Associated Press, August 14, 2004.

Recent Trends in Wealth Ownership and New Series Household Data, jstaff.umkc.edu/jlwae3/workingpapers/geconinequal.pdf

Shaw, Wendy. 1997. The Spatial Concentration of Affluence in the United States. Geographical Review, 87(4), pp. 546–553.

U.S. Bureau of the Census. 1998. Current Populations Report. P60–206.

U.S. Bureau of the Census, Current Population Survey, www.census.gov/hhes/poverty

U.S. Bureau of the Census, Current Population Survey, 1960–2004 Annual Social and Economic Supplements

U.S. Bureau of the Census, Historical Poverty Tables, www.census.gov/hhes/poverty/histpov/hstpov4.html

Watkins, J. 2003. Recent Trends in Wealth Ownership and New Series Household Data. Working paper, University of Missouri at Kansas City, j.staff.umkc.edu/jlwae3/workingpapers/geconinequal.pdf

Wolff, Edward N. 2004. Changes in Household Wealth in the 1980s and 1990s in the U.S. The Levy Economics Institute and New York University. Working Paper No. 407. Online at: www.levy.org/default.asp?view=publications_view&pubID=fca3a440ee

Appalachia

Agency for Toxic Substances and Disease Registry. www.atsdr.cdc.gov/hazdat.html

American Communities Project. browns4.dyndns.org/cen2000_s4/report.html

Appalachian Regional Commission, Online Resource Center, Regional Data and Research, 2002, www.arc.gov/index.do?nodeId=58

Blodgett, Jeff. 2003. Manufacturing on the Ropes: A National Perspective. CT Business Magazine, July/August. www.cerc.com/detpages/services772.html

Centers for Disease Control. 2003. Chronic Disease Overview, 2003, www.cdc.gov/accdhp/overview.htm

Centers for Disease Control, Division of HIVAIDS Prevention. 1999. HIVAIDS Surveillance Report; 1999 Year End Report. Atlanta: Centers for Disease Control and Prevention, 11(2).

Eberhardt M., D. Ingram, and D. Makuc. 2001. Urban and Rural Health Chartbook. Health, United States, 2001. Hyattsville, MD: National Center for Health Statistics.

Fair Data. www.fairdata2000.com

Glasmeier, Amy, Risa Whitson, Lawrence Wood, and Kurt Fuellhart. 2005. Appalachia: Rich in Natural Resource Wealth, Poor in Human Opportunity. With a Geographic View of Pittsburgh and the Alleghenies: Precambrian to Post-Industrial. University of Pittsburgh Press.

Glasmeier, Amy and J. Bradford Jensen. 2001. Entry, Exit, and Restructuring in Appalachian Manufacturing 1963–1992: Evidence from the Longitudinal Research Database. Growth and Change, 32, pp. 251–282.

Delta

Agency for Toxic Substances and Disease Registry. www.atsdr.cdc.gov/hazdat.html

American Communities Project. browns4.dyndns.org/cen2000_s4/report.html

Centers for Disease Control. 2003. Chronic Disease Overview, 2003, www.cdc.gov/accdhp/overview.htm

Centers for Disease Control, Division of HIVAIDS Prevention. 1999. HIVAIDS Surveillance Report; 1999 Year End Report. Atlanta: Centers for Disease Control and Prevention, 11(2).

Colclough, G., and C. Tolbert. 1990. High Technology, Work, and Inequality in Southern Labor Markets. Work and Occupation, 17(1), pp. 3–29.

Eberhardt M., D. Ingram, and D. Makuc. 2001. Urban and Rural Health Chartbook. Health, United States, 2001. Hyattsville, MD: National Center for Health Statistics.

Fair Data. www.fairdata2000.com

Farrigan, Tracey. 2005. The Tunica Miracle, Sin and Savior in America's Ethiopia: A Poverty and Social Impact Analysis of Casino Gambling in Tunica, MS. Unpublished Dissertation, Department of Geography, Pennsylvania State University.

Glasmeier, Amy and Robin Leichenko. 1999. The Transformation of a Rural Region and the Rise of the New South: Miracle or Mirage? In Richard Tardinico (ed.), Poverty or Development? New York: Routledge, pp. 19–40.

HUD Environmental Maps/e-Maps. 198.102.62.140/emaps/searchframe.asp

Lambright, Nsembi. 2001. Community Organizing for School Reform in the Mississippi Delta. Education Policy Center, The Urban Institute.

Rural Community Assistance Partnership (RCAP). 2005. Still Living without the Basics in the 21st Century, www.rcap.org/slwob.html

University of Wisconsin, Eau Claire, Geography 188 course materials, www.uwec.edu/Geography/Ivogeler/w188/south/slavery.htm

First Nation Poverty

Agency for Toxic Substances and Disease Registry. www.atsdr.cdc.gov/hazdat.html

American Communities Project. browns4.dyndns.org/cen2000_s4/report.html

Centers for Disease Control. 2003. Chronic Disease Overview, 2003, www.cdc.gov/accdhp/overview.htm

Centers for Disease Control, Division of HIV/AIDS Prevention. 1999. HIVAIDS surveillance report; 1999 year end report. Atlanta: Centers for Disease Control and Prevention, 11(2).

Fair Data. www.fairdata2000.com

Housing Assistance Council. 2003. Taking Stock of Rural People, Poverty, and Housing for the 21st Century. www.ruralhome.org/pubs/hsganalysis/ts2000/

HUD Environmental Maps/e-Maps. 198.102.62.140/emaps/searchframe.asp

National Indian Gaming Association. 1998. American Indian Gaming Policy and Its Socio-Economic Effects, Report to the National Gambling Impact Study Commission.

indiangaming.org/library/studies/1004-erg_98rept_to_ngisc.pdf

U.S. Bureau of the Census. 1998. Current Populations Report. P60–206.

U.S. Bureau of the Census, Current Population Survey, www.census.gov/hhes/poverty

U.S. Bureau of the Census, Current Population Survey, 1960–2004 Annual Social and Economic Supplements

U.S. Bureau of the Census, Historical Poverty Tables www.census.gov/hhes/poverty/histpov/hstpov4.html

U.S. Department of Health and Human Services, Indian Health Service. 1998. Trends in Indian Health, 1994–1997, www.ihs.gov/publicinfo/archives/#4Publications

U.S. Department of Health and Human Services, Indian Health Service. 1997. Regional Differences in Indian Health, 1994–1996, www.ihs.gov/publicinfo/archives/#4Publications

U.S. Department of the Interior, National Atlas.gov, nationalatlas.gov/fed-landmapwhole.html

Border

Agency for Toxic Substances and Disease Registry. www.atsdr.cdc.gov/hazdat.html

Centers for Disease Control. 2003. Chronic Disease Overview, 2003, www.cdc.gov/accdhp/overview.htm

Centers for Disease Control, Division of HIV/AIDS Prevention. 1999. HIV/AIDS surveillance report; 1999 year end report. Atlanta: Centers for Disease Control and Prevention, 11(2).

Eberhardt M., D. Ingram, and D. Makuc. 2001. Urban and Rural Health Chartbook. Health, United States, 2001. Hyattsville, MD: National Center for Health Statistics.

Fair Data. www.fairdata2000.com

HUD Environmental Maps/e-Maps. 198.102.62.140/emaps/searchframe.asp

Kandel, William and John Cromartie. 2004. New Patterns of Hispanic Settlement in Rural America. Rural Development Research Report No. RDRR99. ERS, U.S. Department of Agriculture.

Newman, Constance. 2004. Growth of Hispanics in Rural Workforce, Amber Waves. U.S. Department of Agriculture, Economic Research Service.

Samuels, Michael, Janice Probst, and Saundra Glover. n.d. Rural Research Focus: Minorities in Rural America. Rural Health Policy. Washington, DC: Health Resources and Services Administration.

Rural

Amber Waves. The USDA Economic Research Service's New Magazine. Selected issues. www.ers.usda.gov/publications/RuralAmerica/archives/

O'Hare, William P. and Kenneth M. Johnson. 2004. Facing Child Poverty in Rural America. www.prb.org/Template.cfm?Section=PRB&template=/ContentManagement/ContentDisplay.cfm&ContentID=11450

Rural Poverty at a Glance. 2004. Economic Research Service, U.S. Department of Agriculture. www.prb.org

Zimmerman, Julie N. 1997. Rural Poverty: Myths and Realities. www.ag.iastate.edu/centers/rdev/newsletter/june97/rural-poverty.html

Segregation

Colclough, G. and C. Tolbert. 1990. High Technology, Work, and Inequality in Southern Labor Markets. Work and Occupations, 17(1), pp. 3–29.

Fair Data. www.fairdata2000.com

Segregated Places, Segregated Spaces: Income and Racial Segregation in America, 1970–2000. Regional Studies. Glasmeier, Amy.

Joint Center for Political and Economic Studies. www.jointcenter.org

Lewis Mumford Center. 2001. Ethnic Diversity Grows, Neighborhood Integration Lags Behind. Washington, DC: Author.

Logan, John. 2002. Choosing Segregation: Racial Imbalance in American Public Schools, 1990–2000. Albany, NY: Lewis Mumford Center for Comparative Urban and Regional Research, University at Albany.

Logan, John, and Deirdre Oakley. 2004. The Continuing Legacy of the Brown Decision: Court Action and School Segregation, 1960–2000. Albany, NY: Lewis Mumford Center for Comparative Urban and Regional Research, University at Albany.

Public Policy Institute. 2001. Hispanics 65 and Older: Sources of Retirement Income. Washington, DC: AARP.

Sampson, R. J. 1997. The Embeddedness of Child and Adolescent Development: A Community-Level Perspective on Urban Violence. In J. McCord (ed.), Violence and Childhood in the Inner City. New York: Cambridge University Press, pp. 61–64.

American Poverty Policy

Boston College Center for Work and Family, Carroll School of Management. 2003. Increasing the Visibility of the Invisible Workforce: Model Programs and Policies for Hourly and Lower Wage Employees. Final Report. Boston: Author.

Danziger, Sheldon H., and Robert Havemen. 2002. Understanding Poverty. Cambridge, MA: Harvard University Press.

Danziger, Sheldon H., and D. H. Weinberg (eds.). 1986. Fighting Poverty: What Works and What Doesn't. Cambridge, MA: Harvard University Press.

Douglas, Paul. 1971. In the Fullness of Time. The Memoirs of Paul H. Douglas. New York: Harcourt Brace Jovanovich.

Haveman, Robert H. 1977. Tinbergen's Income Distribution: Analysis and Policies-A Review Article. Journal of Human Resources, 12(1), pp. 103–114.

Levitan, Sar A. 1973. Programs in Aid of the Poor for the 1970s (Policy Studies in Employment and Welfare, No. 1). Baltimore, MD: Johns Hopkins University Press.

Levitan, Sar A., Wilbur J. Cohen, and Robert J. Lampman. 1968. Towards Freedom From Want. Madison, WI: Industrial Relations Research Association.

Graphical Sources

Tables

1. www.census.gov/hhes/poverty/threshld/thresh04.html

2. www.census.gov/hhes/www/poverty03.html

3–7. www.census.gov/hhes/income/histinc/histpovtb.html

8. www.levy.org/default.asp?view=publications_view&pubID=fca3a440ee

9. www.census.gov/hhes/income/histinc/ineqtoc.html

10. factfinder.census.gov

11. Annie E. Casey Foundation

12–13. factfinder.census.gov

14. www.bls.gov/news.release/wkyeng.t03.htm

15. www.iwpr.org/Employment/Research_employment.htm

16. www.bls.gov/cps/cpswp2003.pdf

17. www.census.gov/population/socdemo/race/black/tabs98/tab09A.txt

18. www.levy.org/default.asp?view=publications_view&pubID=fca3a440ee

19. www.ers.usda.gov/publications/rdrr99

20. www.census.gov/population/www/documentation/twps005

21. www.census.gov/population/socdemo/

22–23. www.bls.gov/cps/wlf-tables23.pdf

24. Author's analysis of Census data

25–28. Poverty Amid Plenty: The American Paradox. The Report of the President's Commission on Income Maintenance Programs. 1966.

29. Appalachian Regional Commission, 2004.

30. Robin Leichenko provided boundaries, published in Accounting for Lower Income Levels in Tribal Areas. USDA ERS.

31. U.S. Department of Education, National Center for Education Statistics, Common Core of Data.

32. indiangaming.org/library/studies/1004-erg_98rept_to_ngisc.pdf

33. Sampson, R. J. 1997. The embeddedness of child and adolescent development: A community-level perspective on urban violence. In J. McCord (ed.), Violence and Childhood in the Inner City. New York: Cambridge University Press.

34–36. browns4.dyndns.org/cen2000_s4/WholePop/WPsort.html

37–39. Danziger, Sheldon H., and D. H. Weinberg (eds.). 1986. Fighting Poverty: What Works and What Doesn't. Cambridge, MA: Harvard University Press.

40–45. Danziger, Sheldon H., and Robert Havemen. 2002. Understanding Poverty. Cambridge, MA: Harvard University Press.

Figures

1. www.epinet.org/content.cfm/books_howmuch

2–3. Author's analysis of Census data

4. www.census.gov/hhes/poverty/poverty02/pov02fig1.jpg

5. Danziger, Sheldon H., and D. H. Weinberg (eds.). 1986. Fighting Poverty: What Works and What Doesn't. Cambridge, MA: Harvard University Press.

6. www.census.gov/hhes/poverty/poverty02/pov02fig4.jpg

7. www.census.gov/hhes/poverty/poverty02/pov02fig6.jpg

8. www.census.gov/hhes/poverty/poverty02/pov02fig2.jpg

9. Author's analysis of Census data

10. www.census.gov/hhes/income/histinc/histpovtb.html

11. AARP. www.aarp.org/research/reference/statistics/aresearch-import-519.html

12. www.census.gov/hhes/income/histinc/histpovtb.html

13. National Center for Health Statistics, National Immunization Survey (Apr.–Dec. 1994–2002)

14. U.S. Department of Education, National Center for Education Statistics, Common Core of Data

15. www.iwpr.org/Employment/Research_employment.htm

16. AARP. www.aarp.org/research/reference/statistics/aresearch-import-519.html

17–18. www.bls.census.gov/

19. www.iwpr.org/Employment/Research_employment.htm

20–21. www.bls.gov/cps/cpswom2003.pdf

22. www.bls.gov/news.release/wkyeng.t03.htm

23–24. www.iwpr.org/Employment/Research_employment.htm

25. Annie E. Casey Foundation

26. www.bls.census.gov/

27. Author's analysis of Census data

28–29. www.sentencingproject.org/

30–32. pewresearch.org/trends/trends2005-hispanic.pdf

33. Kochhar. R. 2004

34–37. AARP. 2002. Beyond 50: A Report to the Nation on Economic Security. Social Security Administration. Income of the Aged Chart Book 2001. Washington, DC: Policy Research Division, AARP.

38–39. www.aarp.org/research/reference/statistics/aresearch-import-519.html

40. txsdc.utsa.edu/maps/thematic/sf3/sf3_10h.php

41. www.aarp.org/research/reference/statistics/aresearch-import-519.html

42–43. www.levy.org/default.asp?view=publications_view&pubID=fca3a440ee

44–51. Author's analysis of Census data

52. Keystone Research Center, Workforce of the Future, Study for the ARC. 2005.

53–60. Graphics based on Census data analyzed by the author

61. www.ihs.gov/publicinfo/archives/#4Publications

62. www.ruralhome.org/pubs/hsganalysis/delta/sacred.htm

63–72. Graphics based on Census data analyzed by the author

73–74. Author's analysis of Census data

75–76. browns4.dyndns.org/cen2000_s4/noresegregation/brown01.htm

77. browns4.dyndns.org/cen2000_s4/HispanicPop/HspReportNew/page1.htm

78–79. Danziger, Sheldon H., and D. H. Weinberg (eds.). 1986. Fighting Poverty: What Works and What Doesn't. Cambridge, MA: Harvard University Press.

Maps

1–4. Author's analysis of Census data

5. Appalachian Regional Commission, special compilation of 1960 Census data. Washington, DC.

6. factfinder.census.gov

7. National Center for Health Statistics, National Immunization Survey (N=25,247 households for Apr.–Dec. 1994–2002)

8. Children's Defense Fund, The State of Children in America's Union, A 2002 Action Guide to Leave No Child Behind

9–10. Annie E. Casey Foundation. www.aecf.org/initiatives/fes/reading/index.htm#ji

11. U.S. Department of Education, National Center for Education Statistics, Common Core of Data.

12–13. Urban Institute and Kaiser Commission on Medicaid and the Uninsured, estimates based on pooled March 2002 and 2003 Current Population Surveys

14. www.iwpr.org/States2004/SWS2004/index.htm

15–16. Author's analysis of data

17. www.sentencingproject.org/

18. Bureau of Justice Statistics. Prison and Jail Inmates at Midyear 2001

19–28. Author's analysis of Census data

29–31. Author's analysis of data from the Annie E. Casey Foundation

32–67. Author's analysis of Census data

68. Map compiled by Philip Kolb from Appalachian Regional Commission data

69. Map compiled by Philip Kolb from USGS data

70–74. Maps based on Census data analyzed by the author

75. Map compiled by Philip Kolb

76–77. www.uwec.edu/Geography/Ivogeler/w188/south/slavery.htm

78. Map based on Agriculture Census data analyzed by the author

79–91. Maps based on Census data analyzed by the author

92. U.S. Department of Education, National Center for Education Statistics, Common Core of Data

93. Compiled by Philip Kolb

94–112. Maps based on Census data analyzed by the author

113–115. mumford1.dyndns.org/cen2000/WholePop/WPsort/sort_d1.html

Photographs

1. www.archives.gov/exhibit_hall/treasures_of_congress/Images/page_19/63a.html

2. www.ohvec.org/galleries/mountaintop_removal/007/

3. www.usda.gov/oc/ photo/99bw0665.htm

Index